CGP GEOGRAPHY RESOURCES

GCSE GEOGRAPHY

The Essential Study Guide (OCR B)

This book perfectly covers the human and physical geography content for the OCR Examining Board, specification B.

The information is explained fully, and written concisely so that each topic can be displayed on a single page.

Contents

Section Four
People, Work and Development

Section Five
Geographical Skills

Published by CGP

Editors:
Kate Houghton
Becky May
Edward Robinson
Rachel Selway

Contributors:
Rosalind Browning, Martin Chester, Simon Cook, Chris Dennett,
Leigh Edwards, Paddy Gannon, Catherine Graley, Dominic Hall, Tim Major,
Barbara Melbourne, Emma Singleton, James Paul Wallis, David Walmsley.
Cover designed by David Rourke

With thanks to Edward Robinson and Angela Ryder for proofreading.

Weather and Climate

<u>Weather</u> is all of the temporary atmospheric conditions found at a place at any one time. Weather shouldn't be confused with <u>climate</u>, which describes the <u>long-term</u> weather conditions most commonly associated with a certain place.

Weather is Made Up of Different __Components__

Weather is made up of a number of <u>components</u> which can change hour-by-hour and day-by-day. The most commonly recorded components are:

- <u>Temperature</u> — how hot or cold the air is.

- <u>Air pressure</u> — the 'weight' of the atmosphere.

- <u>Wind</u> — the horizontal movement of air.

- <u>Cloud</u> — water droplets or ice crystals held in the lower atmosphere.

- <u>Relative humidity</u> — the <u>actual</u> amount of water vapour in the lower atmosphere compared to what it <u>could</u> hold at that temperature.

- <u>Precipitation</u> — water from the atmosphere falling as rain, hail or snow.

There are __Three Main Types__ of Rainfall

Rainfall happens when water in the atmosphere cools. At <u>dew-point</u> the air is <u>saturated</u> and water vapour <u>condenses</u> to form tiny droplets of water which make up <u>cloud</u>. The droplets get bigger until they fall as <u>rain</u>.

<u>Relief rainfall</u> — If warm, wet, onshore winds reach a <u>mountain barrier</u> they have to <u>rise</u> over it. The air <u>cools</u> and <u>condenses</u>. Clouds are formed and precipitation starts. When the air reaches the <u>summit</u> the drier air <u>descends</u>.

The air becomes <u>warmer</u> as it descends and any remaining clouds <u>evaporate</u>. This drier area is known as a <u>rain shadow</u>. Yorkshire is in a rain shadow.

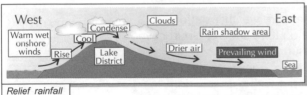

Relief rainfall

<u>Convectional rainfall</u> — The Sun <u>heats</u> the ground and warm air <u>rises</u> vertically. As it rises it <u>cools</u> until <u>condensation point</u> is reached, when thick cumulonimbus clouds are built up by strong thermal up-currents which produce <u>low pressure</u>.

This low pressure causes air to move to the centre — rainfall is heavy and intense and is sometimes accompanied by <u>thunder</u> and <u>lightning</u> due to the electrically unstable conditions. Convectional rainfall occurs all year round in <u>equatorial</u> areas.

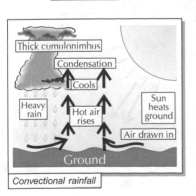

Convectional rainfall

EXAMPLES

Type of rainfall	Where it occurs in the UK
Relief (orographic)	Lake District, Pennines
Convectional	East Anglia
Frontal	All over UK

<u>Frontal rainfall</u> — A <u>low</u> is formed where <u>warm</u> and <u>cold air</u> meet. This causes <u>condensation</u> and <u>frontal rain</u>. This can be <u>light drizzle</u> or <u>heavy rain</u> depending on its <u>position</u> in the low.

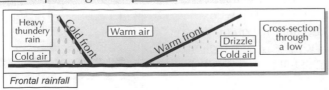

Frontal rainfall

FACT

The UK receives all three types of rainfall. Much of this is due to continual weather depressions or lows that pass over us. See page 5 for more on this.

Measuring and Recording Weather

Weather can be both scientifically recorded and predicted.

Weather is <u>Measured</u> by <u>Weather Instruments</u>

- <u>Temperature</u> is measured by a maximum and minimum <u>thermometer</u> which records the highest and lowest extremes reached each day.

- <u>Pressure</u> is measured using a <u>barometer</u> which gives a reading in <u>millibars</u>. Looking at whether it's rising or falling means you can <u>predict weather</u>.

- <u>Wind speed</u> is measured with an <u>anemometer</u>.

- <u>Wind direction</u> is observed by using a <u>weather vane</u>. The <u>arrow</u> points to where the wind has come <u>from</u>.

- <u>Rainfall</u> is measured using a <u>rain gauge</u>.

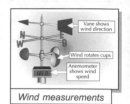

Wind measurements

<u>Synoptic Charts</u> are <u>Weather Maps</u>

Synoptic charts are used to visually represent the information measured by weather instruments.

Synoptic charts are used on TV weather forecasts.

The line from X to Y shows a cross-section of a depression (see page 5).

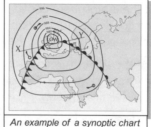

An example of a synoptic chart

EXAM TIP

You can practise reading synoptic charts by using the key on this page to interpret synoptic charts in a newspaper — this will help you learn the symbols for the exam.

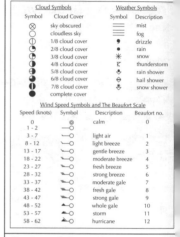

Cloud Symbols		Weather Symbols	
Symbol	Cloud Cover	Symbol	Description
⊗	sky obscured	≡	mist
○	cloudless sky	=	fog
◐	1/8 cloud cover	,	drizzle
◑	2/8 cloud cover	•	rain
◑	3/8 cloud cover	✳	snow
◐	4/8 cloud cover	⚡	thunderstorm
◕	5/8 cloud cover	◦	rain shower
◕	6/8 cloud cover	⊖	hail shower
◑	7/8 cloud cover	⚫	snow shower
●	complete cover		

Wind Speed Symbols and The Beaufort Scale			
Speed (knots)	Symbol	Description	Beaufort no.
0	⊚	calm	0
1 - 2	—○	light air	1
3 - 7	⌐○	light breeze	2
8 - 12	⌐○	gentle breeze	3
13 - 17	⊢○	moderate breeze	4
18 - 22	⊢○	fresh breeze	5
23 - 27	⊨○	strong breeze	6
28 - 32	⊨○	moderate gale	7
33 - 37	⊨○	fresh gale	8
38 - 42	⊨○	strong gale	9
43 - 47	⊨○	whole gale	10
48 - 52	▲○	storm	11
53 - 57	▲○	hurricane	12
58 - 62	▲○		

Key to symbols used in a synoptic chart

Synoptic charts help predict the weather:

All over the UK there are <u>weather stations</u> which collect data on temperature, cloud cover, precipitation, pressure etc. These can be used to draw maps or charts. These can then be studied and compared with past situations to <u>predict</u> the future weather.

The key above tells you how cloud symbols and wind speed are shown on synoptic charts. The two are combined to give a weather station symbol, with the <u>tail angle</u> showing <u>wind direction</u> (shown on the right).

FACT

Atmospheric pressure can range from 890mb in a hurricane (see page 6) to 1060mb in an anticyclone (see page 5).

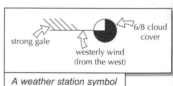

strong gale   6/8 cloud cover
westerly wind (from the west)

A weather station symbol

<u>Synoptic Charts</u> show <u>Atmospheric Pressure Conditions</u>

<u>Atmospheric pressure</u> is: 'the force exerted by the atmosphere as a result of its weight above a unit area of the Earth's surface'. It's measured in <u>millibars</u> (mb) and shown on a weather map or synoptic chart as <u>isobars</u> — lines joining points of <u>equal pressure</u>. <u>Lows</u> and <u>highs</u> are both shown by a series of <u>isobars</u> in a roughly circular shape. Lows have isobar readings which <u>decrease in value</u> towards the centre — highs are the <u>opposite</u>.

EXAM TIP

British weather is largely controlled by weather being high or low pressure — you'll be expected to be able to identify lows and highs on a chart along with the weather linked to them (see page 3).

You also need to know the symbols for <u>fronts</u> (right) which are linked with lows. There's also information on the synoptic chart showing <u>wind direction</u>, <u>cloud cover</u>, <u>temperature</u> and <u>weather</u>.

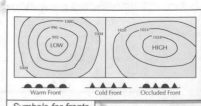

Warm Front   Cold Front   Occluded Front

Symbols for fronts

Identifying Weather Patterns

Nowadays weather maps on TV are pretty accurate. That's because satellites can transmit images taken from a great height above the Earth — giving a good overview of the cloud formations below.

Satellite Images Help us Understand the Weather

A weather satellite

Since the 1960s, satellite images of clouds have been used to <u>predict weather</u>.

These are transmitted to us by satellites orbiting the Earth and give us a good <u>overall view</u> of the world's weather situation.

On visible images, any <u>light surfaces</u> (like clouds) reflect light and appear white whilst <u>dark surfaces</u> (like the sea) appear black.

<u>Infra-red</u> images show the <u>temperature</u> of a surface — the lighter the colour, the colder the temperature is.

Satellite Images are <u>Converted</u> to <u>Synoptic Charts</u>

Images from satellites can be <u>converted</u> into synoptic charts. The warm and cold fronts occur at the <u>edges</u> of the cloud formations. The clouds usually circle around areas of <u>low pressure</u>. The <u>isobars</u> follow the pattern of the clouds.

Below is an infra-red picture transmitted by a satellite orbiting the Earth.

This is the corresponding synoptic chart. It shows all the information given by the satellite in one diagram.

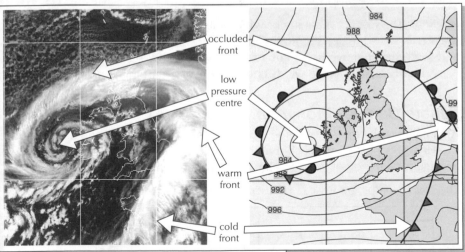

Converting information from a satellite image into a synoptic chart

On images of the UK it's easy to see <u>lows</u> with dense, circular patterns of white cloud along the rain-laden fronts and mottled areas of individual white patches of cloud behind them.

World Climate Zones

Each part of the Earth's surface is classified as belonging to a specific climatic zone, according to the weather conditions most commonly associated with it.

The World has Several *Climatic Zones*

Classification is based on maximum and minimum temperatures and the temperature range, as well as total and seasonal distribution of precipitation.

Because there are so few types of climate in the world and because we can see climatic patterns, there must be some influencing factors at work.

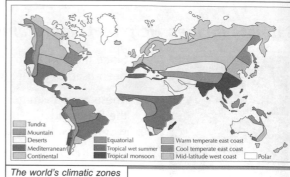

Tundra		
Mountain		
Deserts	Equatorial	Warm temperate east coast
Mediterranean	Tropical wet summer	Cool temperate east coast
Continental	Tropical monsoon	Mid-latitude west coast
		Polar

The world's climatic zones

A Country's *Climate* Depends on *Five Factors*

Latitude: Generally the overall temperature decreases and temperature range increases as you go further from the equator, because the Sun's angle is lower nearer the poles.

Altitude: Generally temperatures decrease where there is an increase in height above sea-level. Upland areas tend to be wetter as well, due to relief rainfall.

Continentality: Places on or near the coast have a smaller temperature range than those inland. This is because land heats up and cools down more quickly than the sea. Inland areas are drier, as wet winds from the sea have lost most of their moisture before they reach here.

Prevailing winds: If these are warm (i.e. they've blown from a hot area) they'll raise the temperature. If they come from colder areas they'll lower it. If they come from the sea (onshore) or a wet area they'll bring rain. If they're offshore or blow over a dry area they'll be dry.

Position: The world has six major wind belts and an area's position relative to these tells us its precipitation (rainfall) characteristics. These belts move north and south with the overhead Sun, causing wet and dry seasons in some areas, like South East Asia, as the winds change direction during the year.

Climate Can be Shown on a *Graph*

A climate graph consists of a line graph showing temperature, and a bar chart showing precipitation for each month of the year. The data used is usually the average for a period of years to eliminate unusual conditions.

The shapes of the graphs can be used to identify different types of climate.

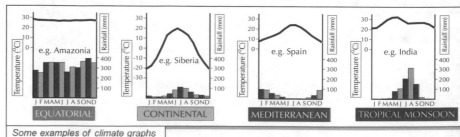

Some examples of climate graphs

Pressure Systems – Lows and Highs

High and low air pressure cause different types of weather.
An island like the UK gets a mixture of highs and lows,
whereas an inland area like Siberia mainly experiences highs.

Lows (Depressions) Cause 75% of UK Weather

Lows (or depressions) form to the west of the UK. Warm, wet tropical maritime air from the south meets cold polar air from the north along the Polar Front.

The warmer, less dense air is forced to rise above the colder air resulting in 'less' air at the Earth's surface. An area of low pressure occurs. This low with its warm and cold fronts moves north-east across the UK bringing an associated pattern of weather conditions with it (see below).

Areas of high pressure are the exact opposite of depressions. There are permanent areas of high pressure between 30° and 40° latitude (the sub-tropical high) and at the two poles.

Lows Bring a Definite Series of Weather Conditions

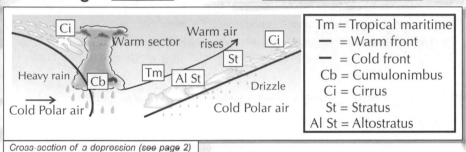

Tm = Tropical maritime
── = Warm front
── = Cold front
Cb = Cumulonimbus
Ci = Cirrus
St = Stratus
Al St = Altostratus

Cross-section of a depression (see page 2)

As a low approaches, it starts to drizzle.
It rains more heavily as the warm front approaches.

When the warm front passes, the rain stops, the weather becomes brighter, and the clouds disappear. The temperature rises, due to being in the warm sector.

The cold air behind the cold front moves faster than the warm air, and often overtakes and undercuts the warm sector, giving an occluded front — no warm sector but a longer period of continuous rainfall.

About 12 hours on, it gets windier and colder. Clouds build up as the cold front moves in. Heavy rain falls and it's cold and windy for the next few hours.

After the rain, conditions may settle for a short while before the next low or high. As the cold front passes, the wind changes direction (veers) from warm southerly to cool north-westerly.

Highs are Linked to Clear Skies

Highs (or anticyclones) usually bring clear skies and stable conditions, lasting for days or weeks.

In summer they're associated with dry, hot (25°C) weather — our 'heat waves'.

In winter the skies can be clear and bright, causing rapid heat loss by radiation at night, and low night temperatures with heavy frosts even though the days are sunny.

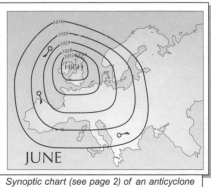

JUNE

Synoptic chart (see page 2) of an anticyclone

Hurricanes

Hurricanes are areas of <u>intense low pressure</u>. They have many names: hurricanes (Atlantic), tropical cyclones (SE Asia), typhoons (Pacific) and willy willies (Australia).

Hurricanes Only Occur in <u>Certain Parts</u> of the World

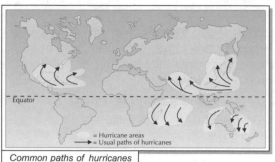

Common paths of hurricanes

= Hurricane areas
→ = Usual paths of hurricanes

Hurricane cloud

Hurricanes start within 8° to 15° north and south of the Equator.
They form over seas when the temperature is higher than 26° C.
They usually occur in <u>late summer</u> and <u>early autumn</u>.
They tend to move <u>westwards</u> once formed and <u>polewards</u> when they reach lan

The <u>Exact Cause</u> of Hurricanes is <u>Uncertain</u>

As they form over warm, moist sea, their <u>energy</u> probably comes from water <u>evaporating rapidly</u> at a <u>high temperature</u>.

The rising air cools and water vapour <u>condenses</u> releasing huge amounts of <u>heat</u> — this heat then provides enough <u>power</u> to drive the storm. Hurricanes rely on plenty of warm, moist air from the <u>sea</u> — they <u>die out</u> over land.

Hurricanes Bring <u>Extreme Weather</u>

A hurricane's life-span is about <u>7 to 14 days</u> — but it's only in one place for a <u>few hours</u>. It's an intense upward spiral or <u>vortex</u> of warm air.

An affected area experiences three main stages of the storm. During the first (A), there will be strong winds and rain.

The central part (B) is called the eye. It's 30 to 50 km across and is produced by <u>descending air</u> — the weather there is <u>calm</u>, with light winds and no rain.

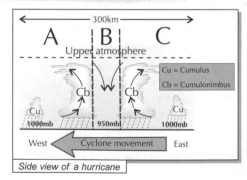

Side view of a hurricane

After the eye has passed, conditions in the final stage (C) are similar to stage A. The winds and rain are strongest in the area immediately <u>surrounding</u> the eye.

	Temperature	Pressure	Wind	Rain
A	Falls	Falls	Very strong >160 km/h	Mid to heavy
B	Rises	Low	Calm, light	None
C	Falls	Rises slowly	As A but opposite direction	Very heavy

FACT

<u>Tornadoes</u> are similar to hurricanes but form over level <u>land</u> areas, e.g. the US plains. A tornado is a violent, whirling vortex of air with a funnel-shaped cloud above. It can cause large-scale damage along a path 150 metres wide and 10 km long.

Effects of Weather on People

A particular example of how <u>weather</u> affects people is the case of a <u>hurricane</u>.

Hurricanes Cause Considerable *Damage*

- <u>High winds</u> can damage buildings, crops, power supplies etc.
- <u>Ocean storm surges</u> can <u>flood</u> coastal areas.
- <u>Heavy rainfall</u> can cause flooding and other damage to homes and crops.

Effects are often <u>more serious</u> in LEDCs than in MEDCs due to lack of emergency services as well as less sturdy houses and higher population density.

Advance Warning of Hurricanes is Now Possible

<u>Up-to-date equipment</u> can track hurricanes to tell us <u>when</u> and <u>where</u> they'll strike next. The USA uses warnings with <u>different levels</u>, e.g. one that there is a 50% chance of a hurricane in the next 36 hours, and another that one is due in the next 12 hours.

These kind of warnings help people to take <u>precautions</u>.

Provisions: food, lighting, first aid. | Protecting houses, turning off gas.

Precautions to take following a hurricane warning

People Need to be Careful During and After the Storm

This is what people are told to do during <u>storms</u>.

<u>During</u> a storm, you should stay <u>inside</u> during the calm period and <u>don't get caught</u> out when the winds and rains start up again. Listen to the <u>radio</u> to keep up-to-date.

<u>After</u> the storm, be <u>careful</u> on damaged roads, and <u>avoid</u> use of water, gas or electricity until the <u>all-clear</u> is given. Report <u>vital damage</u> but <u>don't</u> use the phone unnecessarily.

Climate also Affects Human Lives

<u>Climate</u> and other types of weather can also affect the way we live our lives. Weather affects our day-to-day decisions, such as whether to go out. But climate can have more long-term effects.

- Climate affects where people <u>live</u>. Places with extreme climates, such as deserts and ice-sheets will have few, if any, people living there.

- Climate affects the types of <u>homes</u> people live in. Colder climates need houses with extra <u>insulation</u>. Houses in hot countries often have tiled floors, white walls and shutters, to keep the heat to a <u>minimum</u>.

- <u>Farming</u> is affected by climate and weather. Certain crops only grow in certain climates, and unexpected weather conditions can destroy a harvest.

- <u>Lifestyle</u> is influenced by weather and climate. In hot countries, it's normal to <u>rest</u> through the hottest part of the day and work in the cooler afternoon. <u>Leisure</u> is also influenced by weather, e.g. football matches can be rained off.

- The <u>heat waves</u> caused by high pressure can cause <u>droughts</u> and <u>forest fires</u>. In winter, the same systems can give <u>freezing</u> conditions and dense <u>fogs</u> that hamper airline flights and road traffic.

- Areas with <u>monsoon</u> climates have a spell of hot, dry weather followed by torrential rain sweeping in off the ocean. Disastrous <u>floods</u> can result.

People Affect Weather

The years since 1980 have been the hottest on record. This is thought to be down to human activities which affect the atmosphere and so affect weather.

Urban and Rural Areas have <u>Different Microclimates</u>

A <u>microclimate</u> is where there are <u>local differences</u> in <u>climatic features</u>. This can be due to a variety of reasons linked to local environmental features.

- Urban areas have a <u>higher average</u> temperature than the surrounding countryside — up to 4° C at night and 1.6° C in the day. This is called the '<u>Urban Heat Island Effect</u>'. It happens because buildings act like <u>storage heaters</u> absorbing the Sun's heat during the day and letting it out at night. Also, the air is full of <u>pollutants</u>, which acts as a blanket at night to stop heat getting out. In addition, heat is <u>added</u> to the air from things like central heating, factories and power stations.

- <u>Sunshine levels are lower</u> in urban areas, and there's more <u>cloud</u>, <u>rain</u> and <u>fog</u>, as the high level of pollutant particles in the air act as <u>condensation nuclei</u> (this basically means water forms around them).

- <u>Humidity is higher</u> in urban areas as the warmer air can hold more moisture.

- Wind speed is generally <u>reduced</u> by tall buildings in urban areas. However, a <u>wind tunnel effect</u> can occur, for example if the buildings are in rows. This <u>increases</u> wind speed.

EXAM TIP

Don't worry about all the complex science behind global warming. All you need to know are the main principles of how global warming happens and the consequences of increasing temperatures.

Global Warming is caused by <u>Increased Fossil Fuel Use</u>

Since the <u>industrial revolution</u>, people have needed more <u>energy</u> for work and in the home — this has come from burning more <u>fossil fuels</u>, particularly coal and oil.

This <u>burning</u> releases more <u>carbon dioxide</u> and <u>methane</u> into the atmosphere — these increase what's known as the '<u>greenhouse effect</u>'.

<u>Energy</u> from the <u>Sun</u> passes through the <u>atmosphere</u> as light and <u>warms</u> up the <u>Earth</u>. When the energy is radiated and <u>reflected</u> back off the surface as <u>heat</u>, it is <u>trapped</u> by the atmosphere and <u>can't get back out</u> into space — this is like how a <u>greenhouse</u> keeps the heat inside. Increasing the greenhouse gases increases the greenhouse effect, which means the Earth gets <u>hotter</u>.

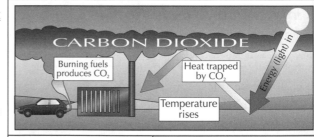

CARBON DIOXIDE

Burning fuels produces CO₂

Heat trapped by CO₂

Energy (light) in

Temperature rises

The greenhouse effect in action

FACT

Global warming is causing sea levels to rise as the increased temperature melts ice sheets and glaciers. This means that most coastal towns are at risk of flooding, including many of the world's major cities like London and New York (see page 17).

There's <u>Conflict</u> Over Reducing <u>Greenhouse Gases</u>

To prevent further global warming, greenhouse gas emissions need to be <u>reduced</u>, but some countries disagree over whether to, for different reasons:

- <u>Britain</u> and <u>Europe</u> use fossil fuels but want to <u>reduce</u> gas emissions.

- <u>India</u> and other <u>LEDCs</u> don't want to reduce emissions because their <u>rate of development</u> would <u>slow down</u>.

- <u>Oil states</u>, e.g. those in the Gulf, don't want to reduce emissions because their <u>revenues</u> from <u>oil sales</u> would <u>go down</u>.

- The <u>USA</u> is reluctant to reduce emissions because it doesn't want a fall in <u>living standards</u>.

Case Studies

You need to know two case studies where extreme
weather conditions have created hazards for people.

Case Study 1: *The Bangladesh Cyclone Disaster, 1991*

Bangladesh is one of the world's most <u>densely populated</u> and <u>poorest</u> countries.
125 million people live in about half the space of the UK. It is situated at the
head of the Bay of Bengal. Three rivers, the Ganges, the Brahmaputra and the
Meghna meet here in a giant low-lying <u>delta</u>. The land is barely 1.5 metres
above sea level in this area and floods are an annual event.

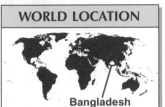

KEY TERM

A <u>delta</u> is a low-lying,
flat area of alluvial
deposition, at the
mouth of a river.

In 1991, a <u>tropical cyclone</u> caused a
major disaster along the south-east
coast and in the delta region.
Winds of over 200 km/h created a
7m high <u>tidal wave</u>. The wave
submerged the coastal districts killing
approximately 125,000 people.

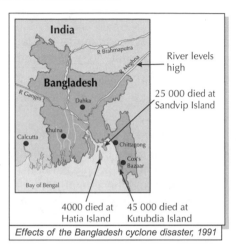

Effects of the Bangladesh cyclone disaster, 1991

There was widespread destruction.

- Roads, bridges, electricity supplies,
  crops and animals were all lost.

- Drinking water was <u>polluted</u> with
  the dirty floodwater and <u>salt water</u>
  contaminated the farmland.
  Damage was estimated
  at over £1 billion.

WORLD LOCATION

Bangladesh

- For survivors, there was a risk of <u>cholera</u> and other diseases due to water
  being contaminated with sewage and dead bodies.

- There was also a risk of <u>starvation</u> in remote areas which aid
  couldn't easily reach.

- The cyclone struck just before the <u>harvest</u>, so food reserves were low,
  and future reserves were destroyed.

Case Study 2: *Drought in the Sahel Region of Africa*

The <u>Sahel</u> region runs across the continent of Africa from east to west. It is
located to the south of the Sahara Desert, containing some of the world's poorest
countries — Sudan, Chad, Niger and Mali. The people are mostly <u>nomadic</u>,
meaning they move from place to place, trying to secure a living from the land.

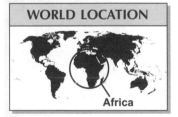

WORLD LOCATION

Africa

For a long time, the Sahel had periods of adequate rainfall, but <u>drought</u> has
become an increasing problem as rain occurs less and less. Continued <u>hot, dry
air</u> blows from the strong <u>high pressure</u> over the desert regions in the north. This
has led to <u>degradation</u> of the land and an advance southwards of desert sands.

The nomadic people have <u>migrated</u> south with their livestock as the formerly
habitable land continues to <u>deteriorate</u>:

- The increasing population has put pressure on the fragile <u>ecosystem</u>.

- Trees have been <u>stripped</u> and completely removed for firewood.

- Grazing and farming have broken up the poor <u>soils</u>, which are easily
  <u>eroded</u> by the wind.

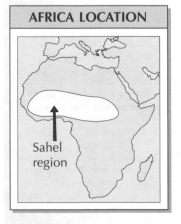

AFRICA LOCATION

Sahel
region

As the land now supports little life, many of the nomadic people have moved
away to the <u>cities</u> where they have added to the problems of <u>overcrowding</u> there.

Ecosystems

Ecosystems are all the living and non-living things sharing a certain environmen[t]

An Ecosystem is a System of Linked Parts

The linked parts of an ecosystem (e.g. animals, plants and their habitats) interact in the ecosystem in a series of <u>inputs</u>, <u>outputs</u>, <u>stores</u>, <u>flows</u>, <u>processes</u> and <u>cycles</u>. A <u>tropical rainforest</u> (TRF) ecosystem has these links:

- The main input is heat and light from the <u>Sun</u>.
  The Sun also triggers a cycle of activity that leads to <u>rainfall</u>.

- The weather (sun and rain) sustains the dense <u>vegetation</u> of the rainforest.

- The rainforest's continuing leaf fall builds up a carpet of <u>debris</u> which decays to provide <u>nutrients</u> for fresh growth.

- <u>Animals</u> and <u>insects</u> help with the scattering of seeds, the pollination of plants and the decay of leaf litter.

- Rainforest plants are <u>eaten</u> by insects, birds and animals, which are in turn eaten by larger animals. Native rainforest <u>people</u> eat both the plants and the animals, in <u>harmony</u> with the ecosystem, not taking more than they need.

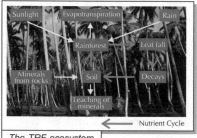

The TRF ecosystem

A Food Chain is a Series of Links in an Ecosystem

Most food chains start with <u>green plants</u> which are called <u>primary producers</u> as they use the Sun's energy to <u>photosynthesise</u>, i.e. make their food.

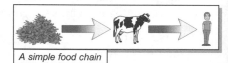

A simple food chain

This is the <u>word equation</u> for photosynthesis:

$$\boxed{\text{Carbon Dioxide}} + \boxed{\text{Water}} + \boxed{\text{Sunlight}} = \boxed{\text{Starch and Sugar}} + \boxed{\text{Water}} + \boxed{\text{Oxygen}}$$

Plants also take up <u>minerals</u> (from rock breakdown) from the <u>soil</u>. Some animals known as <u>herbivores</u> eat these plants. Other animals known as <u>carnivores</u> eat the herbivores and other carnivores.

<u>Organisms die</u> and nutrients return to the soil when bacteria and fungi <u>decompose</u> (break down) the dead material making it ready for <u>re-use</u>. This means the process goes in a <u>cycle</u>.

There are Two Main Natural Cycles in an Ecosystem

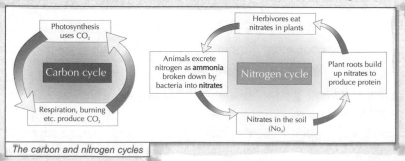

The carbon and nitrogen cycles

Ecosystems as Resources

Ecosystems can be tiny or huge. Whatever the scale, people are part
of ecosystems — we interact with plants, animals and even soil.
We use and affect other parts of ecosystems for our own benefit.

Ecosystems Happen at a _Range of Scales_

The inter-relationships that exist between a set of living organisms, both plant
and animal, and their non-living environment can exist at a range of scales.

A pond, for example, can be seen as an ecosystem in itself. Each component
of the pond's environment, living or non-living, is linked together and interacts.

On a bigger scale, a biome is a region of the Earth that experiences a particular
climate, generating its own vegetation type.

Whatever the scale, the following components can normally be observed:

EXAM TIP

See page 12 for examples
of ecosystems at
different scales.

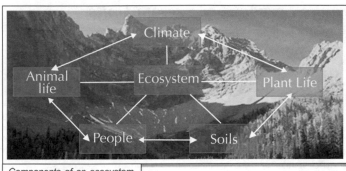

Components of an ecosystem

Ecosystems can be Seen as _Resources_

Resources are things that people use. Because extensive use is made of all
aspects of an ecosystem, ecosystems can be seen as resources.

Rocks and soils provide mineral wealth and the basis for agriculture.
Plants and animals can also be used for a range of products including food.

Savanna Grasslands are a Useful Type of Ecosystem

Savanna grassland is an example of a type of ecosystem
that's used as a resource (see more about the physical
features of savanna grassland on page 12).
Savanna grassland has a number of human land uses:

- Arable farming — vegetation is burned and cleared
  to make room for crops like millet and maize.

- Cattle farming — cows graze on the grass.

- Cash cropping — large expanses of land are used
  to grow things like tobacco and cotton.

- Logging — for fuel and building materials.

- Tourism — people go on safaris to see animals like
  zebras, giraffes, elephants, antelopes and lions.

Arable farming — maize

Cash cropping — cotton

Tourism — safaris

Savanna land uses

EXAMPLES

The Masai Mara national
park in Kenya and the
Serengeti in Tanzania are
examples of areas of
savanna grassland.
These areas are carefully
managed, but are being
negatively affected
by tourism.

Different Sized Ecosystems

Ecosystems exist at a range of <u>scales</u>, from a plant in a pot to a whole forest.

A <u>Pond</u> is an Example of a Small Ecosystem

A <u>pond</u> can be seen as an <u>ecosystem</u> as it is a self-contained environment where living things exist and interact. Within a pond, there is a <u>carbon cycle</u>, <u>nitrogen cycle</u> and <u>food web</u>. Ponds support many species of <u>animal</u>, from bacteria, to insects, to fish, amphibians and even large fish-eating birds such as kingfishers and herons.

The plant life of a pond is also quite diverse. There will be <u>algae</u> and <u>mosses</u> growing on the water's surface, and water-loving plants like <u>pondweed</u> either growing on the surface or totally submerged. The edges of the pond may also support <u>marsh plants</u> like bullrushes and reeds.

The pond ecosystem

<u>Biomes</u> are the Largest <u>Ecosystem Units</u>

This map shows <u>nine</u> <u>biomes</u> — some maps show more or fewer.

As with world climates this is a small number and suggests there are certain key <u>influencing</u> <u>factors</u> — like <u>climate</u>, <u>relief</u>, <u>geology</u> and <u>soils</u>.

- Tropical forests
- Temperate deciduous forests
- Coniferous forests
- Deserts
- Temperate grasslands
- Savanna (tropical) grasslands
- Mediterranean
- Tundra
- Mountains

Distribution of the world's nine different biomes

<u>Savanna Grassland</u> is found North and South of TRFs

These areas have <u>wet</u> and <u>dry seasons</u>. <u>Grasses</u> are spiky and tall (up to 3 metres), e.g. pampas grass — growing in <u>clumps</u> with bare earth between, and dying down in the dry season. Scattered bushes and trees have <u>adapted</u> to cope with the dry season. Some have <u>swollen stems</u> to store water and <u>long root</u> <u>systems</u> to reach the water table. Others have <u>thorny leaves</u> to reduce water loss.

? This is a <u>plagioclimax</u> community, where humans have affected natural cycles and altered natural vegetation. Fire occurs naturally (due to <u>lightning</u>) so mature trees have <u>fire-resistant bark</u>, but more often fires are started by humans to produce cleared land for <u>pasture</u> — so many trees don't have time to mature.

Savanna grassland is a very <u>fragile</u> environment — overgrazing and overcultivation leave the land <u>bare</u>. The bare soil then dries out, erodes and turns into <u>desert</u>. Desertification can be prevented by <u>sustainable</u> farming (see p.81).

<u>Deserts</u> Do Have Enough Rainfall for Some Vegetation

Deserts aren't habitable or farmable — they <u>lack water</u> and <u>rainfall varies</u> from year to year. However, some plants survive in <u>semi-desert</u>:

- <u>small, thorny leaves</u> reduce water loss
- <u>long roots</u> reach deep water supplies
- <u>swollen stems</u> store water (cactus)
- <u>thick waxy skin</u> reduces water loss.

<u>Flowering plants</u>, on the other hand, only take a <u>few days</u> to grow, flower and seed again

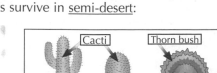
Cacti | Thorn bush
Long roots
Desert plants

EXAMPLES

Savanna grassland

South America e.g. south-east Brazil
Africa e.g. Kenya and Tanzania

Deserts

Africa e.g. Ethiopia, Sudan, Chad, Niger (Sahara desert)
South-west USA e.g. Nevada
Central Australia

EXAMPLES

Savanna plants

Baobab
Pampas grass

Desert plants

Cactus
Thorn bush

Changing Ecosystems: TRFs

Ecosystems can change both by natural processes and human activity. The large-scale removal of trees is one example of how humans can change ecosystems. It is a problem in many TRFs, like the Amazon rainforest in Brazil.

Trees in Brazil are Disappearing for <u>Five</u> Reasons

- <u>Logging</u> for export to MEDCs — trees should be <u>replanted</u> so the industry can keep selling <u>long-term</u>, but many LEDCs want to make money today and don't plant for the future.

- <u>Population</u> is <u>increasing</u> — <u>settlement</u> and <u>road-building</u> in the TRF is needed.

- The forest is cleared to set up <u>cattle ranches</u> which quickly make land useless.

- <u>Mineral extraction</u> helps Brazil pay <u>foreign debts</u> — Carajas in Brazil is the world's largest iron reserve.

- <u>Hydro-electric power</u> has led to large areas of land being <u>flooded</u> (see p.26).

EXAMPLE

Deforestation in Brazil

There are Two Sides to the <u>Deforestation Debate</u>:

For Conservation	For Deforestation
• <u>Agricultural development</u> is pointless — soils robbed of TRF lose fertility, so farming can't continue after three or four years.	• <u>Poverty</u> means a country needs to use all resources to help its people.
• <u>Medicinal products</u> could be destroyed before they're discovered (see page 14).	• Many <u>MEDCs</u> destroyed their <u>own forests</u> when developing — the UK did (although not so fast) — so they shouldn't have one rule for themselves and one for LEDCs who need to develop.
• <u>Heritage value</u> means preserving this ecosystem for future generations — there are many native tribes whose way of life is being destroyed.	• Nearly 75% of world carbon dioxide emissions comes from <u>MEDCs</u> — why should LEDCs have to change policy first?
• Removing the forest means more <u>global warming</u> (see page 14).	• MEDCs should <u>lower interest</u> or <u>cancel debts</u> if they're so worried about deforestation (see page 14).
• Forest removal lowers <u>evapotranspiration</u> (a plant process that gives out water) and rainfall — altering the climate.	• MEDCs are <u>buying</u> the products of these areas — so why should LEDCs stop?

<u>Malaysia</u> sets an example — it exports <u>one third</u> of the world's <u>hardwoods</u> and the government has <u>strict controls</u>. <u>Trees</u> have to be a <u>certain age</u> and <u>height</u> before they're felled and <u>companies</u> must <u>replant</u> as many trees as they remove.

EXAMPLE

Since 1970, western Siberia has produced **oil** and **natural gas**. **Coniferous forests** were **felled** to pave the way for exploration. **Oil spills** have polluted water and land, and there have been **fires**. It's feared the ecosystem **won't** recover — plants take a long time to **re-establish** in such a cold, severe climate.

<u>Deforestation</u> Affects the <u>Structure</u> of the TRF

The TRF is a very <u>fragile</u> environment, and deforestation starts a chain of events affecting the <u>processes</u> and <u>stability</u> of the ecosystem:

- The felling of trees cuts off the <u>nutrient</u> supply to the now exposed soil.
- The heavy daily rainfall easily <u>washes away</u> the now loose, crumbly soil.
- The <u>rivers</u> get blocked with red silty material, which causes <u>flooding</u>.
- Where the soil remains intact, nutrients are washed down into the earth (<u>leached</u>), out of the reach of plants or crops.
- The soil becomes <u>infertile</u> and supports little growth.
- <u>Evaporation</u> and <u>evapotranspiration</u> are reduced by deforestation, so <u>rainfall</u> in the area is reduced, also making plant growth less likely.

EXAMPLES

Other ecosystems are changing too. In the UK, hedgerows and woodland have been removed to make room for farmland. This has destroyed the natural ecosystems of those areas.

Effects of Ecosystem Change: TRFs

Deforestation has a direct impact on people, both within and outside the forest ecosystem, causing both benefits and problems.

The People of the TRF Experience Benefits and Problems

Benefits of Deforestation:
Most rainforest is located in LEDCs such as Brazil and Indonesia.
The money earned from exporting timber, mining and commercial farming as well as other projects would benefit the country as it seeks to become wealthier. Many LEDCs have large debts to MEDCs and the income could help pay them.

The quality of life of the local people is improved if they can get jobs in these new industries, or benefit from the increased wealth of the country.

Problems of Deforestation:
Deforestation affects the soil of the TRF, leaving it barren and infertile (see page 13). Farmers will have a maximum of three years growth from the remaining nutrients after deforestation. When soil is exhausted, it has to be left to recover.

Exposed soil is soon lost, washed into rivers. The sediment clogs up the river channels and often causes flooding. Navigation becomes very difficult, fishing is ruined and water supply is polluted.

Fresh water may be polluted

The native people of the forest often lose their traditional livelihoods, their homes and even their culture. Newcomers to the area can bring diseases with them which can take a large toll on the native people who have no immunity to them.

People Outside the TRF Ecosystem are Also Affected

The effects of deforestation can spread beyond the ecosystem itself.

Benefits of Deforestation:
Clearing areas of forest lets farmers and forestry and mining companies produce primary products that MEDCs need for their economies. Many of these products can be bought in large quantities and at very reasonable prices to be processed and manufactured into goods for MEDC markets.

Problems of Deforestation:
The primary products from cleared TRFs will eventually run out — the mineral deposits will run out and farmland will become too infertile to grow crops.

Medicines have been developed from plants found in the TRF. Deforestation may mean the loss of existing supplies as well as an end to research for more cures.

New species of plant and animal life are still being discovered in the rainforest ecosystem, but continuing destruction will mean the end to such research.

Deforestation seems to be influencing climate on a global scale. Rainfall in the tropics has reduced in volume. On the TRF margins, dry seasons are getting longer and longer. Drought is also becoming a real problem. This is because:

- Trees absorb carbon dioxide from the atmosphere. Deforestation will lead to more carbon dioxide remaining in the atmosphere, adding to concerns over global warming.

- TRF is often cleared through burning. This produces even more carbon dioxide to add to the global warming problem.

EXAMPLE

Deforestation in Nepal affects Bangladesh:

From 1945 to 1985, Nepal in the Himalayas removed half its forests to give land to the growing population. Because it is a mountainous country, this caused large-scale soil erosion. Material was washed into the River Ganges which starts here. The Ganges' bed was raised, increasing flooding risks in the delta area in Bangladesh.

Cleared forest in Nepal

Ecosystem Management: TRFs

It is difficult to find a compromise between exploiting and sustaining ecosystems.

The World's Forest Ecosystems are <u>Disappearing</u> Fast

Forests all over the world are being destroyed for wood, redevelopment, fossil fuels, and farming. <u>Twelve million</u> hectares of the world's forests disappear <u>every year</u>. That's an area half the size of the UK lost every year and it's getting <u>worse</u>.

This has been known about for a long time. The problem is getting people to change their use of forests when it means making <u>less money</u> in the short-term.

The <u>Five</u> Big <u>Sustainable</u> Forestry Techniques

<u>Cabling</u> — Most forestry is done by <u>clear cutting</u>, which is just ploughing into the forest and cutting down lots of trees you don't want to get to the ones you do. <u>Cabling</u>, or <u>heli-logging</u>, is where you air-lift trees out by <u>helicopter</u>, which reduces the amount of needless destruction.

<u>Replanting</u> — Replacing trees that are cut down. More and more <u>laws</u> insist that logging companies do this nowadays. It's important that the right <u>kinds</u> of trees are planted — planting rubber trees instead of a whole load of different rainforest species isn't good enough.

<u>Zoning</u> — Identifying areas (or zones) for different uses. Different areas are set aside for things like tourism, forestry and mining. Some zones are set up as <u>national parks</u> to protect the forest <u>ecosystem</u>.

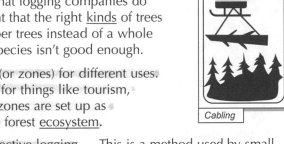
Cabling

FACT

Deforestation has been happening for many centuries. When the Greek and Roman civilisations developed, many natural forests were cleared to make space for farming and settlement. Little natural woodland still exists today, but has been replaced by scrub instead.

Trucks cause damage

<u>Selective logging</u> — This is a method used by small, <u>environmentally sound</u> logging businesses. Only <u>selected trees</u> are chopped — most trees are left standing. Some of the best trees are left standing to maintain a strong <u>gene pool</u>. The least intrusive form is '<u>horse logging</u>' — dragging felled trees out of the forest using horses instead of huge trucks.

<u>Natural regeneration</u> — This means leaving areas of forest to recover <u>naturally</u> before removing trees again.

EXAMPLE

Another example of the destruction of an ecosystem is overfishing — leading to the destruction of natural marine ecosystems. A sustainable approach to fishing is to use nets with a bigger mesh. This means that only the biggest fish are caught, so the fish population doesn't decline.

There's a <u>Three Pronged Attack</u> on Bad Forestry

<u>Promoting sustainable use of the forests</u>

- Creating a <u>demand</u> for sustainable products. Clearly <u>labelling</u> products from '<u>sustainably managed forests</u>'.

- Encouraging <u>small scale projects</u> — e.g. the Body Shop buying ground nut oil from small scale projects run by locals.

- Encouraging <u>ecotourism</u> by advertising and education.

Saving Forests

<u>Discouraging bad practice</u>

- <u>Banning</u> wood from forests that are managed non-sustainably.

- <u>Preventing</u> illegal logging and enforcing protected areas.

- Putting <u>pressure</u> on businesses to only buy from sustainable forests.

FACT

Deforestation has played a part in the elimination of many native groups. For example, 96% of native forest-living people in Brazil have died since the arrival of Europeans. Many died from western diseases which they had no immunity to.

<u>Reducing the need for large scale deforestation</u>

- <u>Debt-for-nature swaps</u> — some of the countries' debt can be bought back by governments or conservation organisations in return for increased commitment to conservation projects.

Case Study

The Amazon Basin of Brazil is an example of a tropical rainforest ecosystem.
Learn this case study of its physical features and the human activities done ther

Case Study: *The Amazon Basin Ecosystem, Brazil*

Climate:

The climate is dominated by <u>high temperatures</u> all year round. The average
temperature is about 26° C, a figure which only varies by 2 or 3 degrees
over the year. This means there is a <u>continuous</u> growing season.

<u>Rainfall</u> is high at more than 2000 mm a year. It generally falls <u>all year</u> round,
although further from the equator, towards the edge of the forest, there is a
short dry season. The high <u>humidity</u> in the forest area means that it rains
heavily every day, usually in the afternoon.

Vegetation:

The vegetation is dominated by <u>deciduous</u>
trees, constantly growing and shedding
leaves at different times. There are no
obvious <u>seasons</u>, so flowers, fruits and
seeds are available all year round.

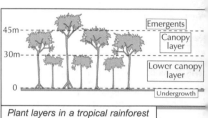

Plant layers in a tropical rainforest

AMERICAN LOCATION

Amazon River

Brazil

The trees form three distinctive <u>layers</u>. The emergent tallest trees
are over 45 metres in height. The <u>canopy layer</u> lies below at about
30 metres. Below that is a thinner, <u>lower</u> canopy. There is only
sparse <u>undergrowth</u> as little light gets through the tree layers.

The trees grow <u>shallow roots</u> and a broad spread of <u>buttress roots</u>
develops above the ground. These give added stability. Leaves are
thick and <u>waxy</u>, cutting down on moisture loss through transpiration.
They also have <u>drip-tips</u> to help the heavy daily rainfall run off quickly.

Soils:

Brazil's tropical rainforest

Soils are mainly red and rather clay-like. They are rich in
iron and aluminium oxides which are left after the heavy rai
has <u>leached</u> out other materials and nutrients. The soil itsel
is largely <u>infertile</u> when the nutrients stored in the biomass
are removed. The poor, loose structure is easily washed awa
when exposed to the heavy rains.

A thick carpet of fallen, decaying <u>leaves</u> builds up on the
forest floor. It rapidly <u>decomposes</u> due to humid conditions
and decomposing bacteria, and makes a <u>fertile</u> top layer of
soil. So despite the poor soil underneath, there are plenty o
nutrients available in the top layer for the dense vegetation.

People:

Some native people are <u>hunter-gatherers</u>, while a larger number live by a form o
<u>shifting cultivation</u> which involves cutting small farming areas into the forest.
Shifting cultivation, or 'slash and burn', is <u>wasteful</u> as the plots are only of any
value for a few years before the soil loses <u>fertility</u> and is <u>eroded</u>. The farmers
move on to repeat the process nearby.

There is pressure from logging, mining, electrical power schemes and
commercial crop production in the forest, so <u>deforestation</u> is happening.
This is a problem for both the <u>environment</u> and the <u>native people</u> who are being
forced out of their homes.

Global warming and acid rain will destroy some of the world's ecosystems, unless something is done to prevent this from happening.

Global Warming Causes *Rising Sea Levels*

Global warming is causing ice-sheets and glaciers to begin to melt. This has caused sea levels to rise by 0.25 m in the last 100 years — and they will probably rise another 0.5 m in the next 100 years. This is putting low lying areas of the world under threat of flooding.

The future?

Global Warming Causes the *World's Climates to Change*

- Droughts, floods and storms could get more severe, widespread and common.
- The northern hemisphere wheat belt could get more arid and less productive.
- The tundra could get warmer and support crop growth.
- The Sahara could spread north into southern Europe.
- The North Atlantic drift (a major ocean current) could be altered, and Britain could get much colder.

Acid Rain comes from *Burning Fossil Fuels*

Acid rain is basically rain which has a higher than normal acid level (i.e. a low pH). Burning coal, oil and natural gas in power stations gives off sulphur dioxide gas. Burning petrol and oil in vehicle engines gives off nitrogen oxides as gases.

These gases mix with water vapour and rain water in the atmosphere, producing weak solutions of sulphuric and nitric acids — which fall as acid rain.

The formation of acid rain

Acid Rain *Damages* Nature and Buildings

- Leaves and tree roots can die from the poison in the rain.
- High acid levels make rivers and lakes unsuitable for fish.
- 'Leaching' increases, which removes nutrients from soils. Crop yields lower.
- Some of the nutrients which get into rivers and lakes can kill the plant and animal life. This overload of nutrients is called 'eutrophication'.
- Acid rain dissolves the stonework and mortar of buildings.

Lime can reduce the effects of acid rain when added to rivers, lakes and soils by neutralising acids — but it's expensive and doesn't always work.

Global Cooperation is Needed

Acid rain and global warming are of international concern — if the ice caps melt, it will be a global problem. Technology can be developed to help:

- Energy companies can burn low sulphur fuel, fit chimney filters or even burn natural gas with its lower level of emissions.
- New cars can be fitted with catalytic converters to cut nitric oxide emissions. Early trials with electric and lean-burn engines have been successful.

Many of these technologies are expensive and need global cooperation. To ensure lasting and effective change, there has to be clear government policy and international agreement. A number of summits have taken place but some nations, like the USA, have been reluctant to sign treaties and commit to policies.

Case Study

You need to know a case study about how acid rain affects a particular place.

Case Study: Acid Rain in <u>Norway</u>

Norway suffers mainly from acid rain that's created elsewhere:

95% of sulphur depositions and 86% of nitrogen-based depositions in Norway come from <u>trans-boundary acid rain</u>, mainly from the UK, Germany and Poland

WORLD LOCATION

Norway

Prevailing southerly <u>winds</u> carry the pollutant clouds across the North Sea from the UK. The air is forced to rise as it reaches the Norwegian coast and the high mountains immediately inland. This results in heavy <u>relief rain</u> and snowfall over the high mountains. pH values of <u>4.5</u> are regularly recorded.

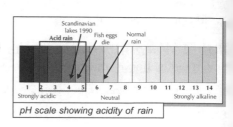

pH scale showing acidity of rain

EUROPEAN LOCATION

The acid rain has terrible effects:

- Norway suffers from the '<u>forest death</u>' syndrome, where many of the trees in its mainly <u>coniferous</u> forests are being killed by acid rain. The problem is worst in the <u>southern</u> counties like Agder, Teleman and Rogaland, where up to 90% of forests are affected.

Dark appearance of an acidified lake

- Many of Norway's <u>streams</u>, <u>rivers</u> and <u>lakes</u> are now so <u>acidic</u> that little or <u>no life</u> is supported. All the lakes in an area of 13 000 km² in the south of the country are devoid of fish and 80% of the country's total number of lakes are either 'dead' (i.e. support no life) or are rapidly reaching this situation.

- The acidification of lakes has been catastrophic for <u>freshwater fish stocks</u>, which has negatively impacted on the people who earn their living from selling these fish.

- The <u>corrosion of buildings</u> costs Norway millions of pounds each year in repairs and threatens some of their heritage as historical buildings in towns like Oslo are affected.

Norway is trying to improve its situation:

Norwegian environmental agencies combat the acid rain by <u>liming</u> affected areas, but this is a major drain on the agencies' finances. So, despite the fact that it's not responsible for most of its acid rain pollution, Norway is aiming to reduce its own <u>sulphur</u> and <u>nitrogen</u> emissions to try and help the situation.

It's using various strategies, including:

- Charging <u>increased tax</u> on sulphur found in oil and sulphur and nitrogen used in industrial processes.

- Enforcing stricter regulations on <u>transport emissions</u>.

These efforts have had some positive results. In 1985, 30% of Norway was experiencing sulphur and nitrogen depositions <u>beyond the critical load</u> of what the land could cope with. In 1990 this had dropped to 25%, and Norway aims to reduce this to <u>only 11%</u> of the land exceeding the critical load by <u>2010</u>.

This first section isn't over until you've been through some questions to see how much you know. When you've finished, do them again, and keep trying them until you can do them all without needing to peek at the book.

1) Name six different components of weather.

2) Explain the difference between relief, convectional and frontal rainfall.

3) Draw the weather symbol for a strong easterly breeze with 7/8 cloud cover.

4) What is atmospheric pressure?

5) What do lows look like on a satellite image?

6) Draw the symbol for an occluded front.

7) Name six climatic zones, and describe roughly where they are in the world.

8) What five factors does a country's climate depend on?

9) Describe the series of weather conditions brought by highs and lows.

10) Describe where highs and lows form.

11) What is the probable cause of hurricanes?

12) Describe the three stages you would experience if a hurricane passed over you.

13) Describe three ways in which weather or climate affect human lives.

14) Why are the effects of hurricanes more serious in LEDCs than in MEDCs? Describe the kinds of damage caused.

15) What is the 'Urban Heat Island Effect'?

16) Explain how global warming occurs.

17) Write a mini-essay on the Bangladesh cyclone disaster.

18) What factors have led to land deteriorating in the Sahel region of Africa?

19) What is the main input of a TRF ecosystem?

20) Describe the two main cycles in an ecosystem.

21) Name the six components which can normally be found in an ecosystem.

22) What are the human land uses of savanna grasslands?

23) Name six of the world's biomes, and describe roughly where they are found.

24) How have desert plants adapted to their harsh environment?

25) Write a mini-essay to discuss both sides of the deforestation debate.

26) How does deforestation affect the structure of the TRF?

27) Compare deforestation's benefits and problems for the people of the TRF.

28) How might deforestation eventually lead to drought?

29) Name five sustainable forestry techniques.

30) Describe the three-pronged attack on bad forestry.

31) Where are tropical rainforests found?

32) Describe the vegetation and soils of the Amazon Basin.

33) How is acid rain created?

34) What effects has acid rain had on Norway?

The Hydrosphere

The <u>hydrosphere</u> is the watery part of the Earth's surface (e.g. oceans, rivers and water vapour in the atmosphere). The system that links all the components of the hydrosphere together is the <u>water cycle</u>.

Evaporated Sea Water Forms the <u>Inputs</u> to the System

The <u>water cycle</u> is the circulation of water between the sea, land and atmosphere. The system starts when <u>clouds</u> of evaporated sea water blow towards land where they rise, causing precipitation like rain, snow or hail to fall on the ground below.

Then the Water <u>Flows</u> Through the System via <u>Transfers</u>

There are two kinds of transfer you need to know about — <u>vertical</u> and <u>horizontal</u>.

<u>Vertical Transfers:</u>
* Water <u>collects</u> on plant leaves — this is called <u>interception</u>. Then it drips off and enters the soil. It can then <u>filter through</u> spaces in the surface layers of the soil — this is called <u>infiltration</u>.

* The water can also <u>move through</u> saturated ground below the water table — this is called <u>percolation</u>.

<u>Horizontal Transfers:</u>
* <u>Surface run-off</u> is when water flows overground to rivers, lakes or the sea.

* <u>Channel flow</u> is the flow of water in a stream, river or lake.

* <u>Through flow</u> is when <u>infiltrated water</u> moves through <u>soil</u> to a river.

* <u>Groundwater flow</u> is when <u>percolated water</u> moves below the water table to a river.

Some Water is <u>Stored</u> in the System

There are <u>four</u> kinds of <u>storage</u> that you need to know about:
* <u>Channel storage</u> happens in <u>rivers</u> and <u>lakes</u> and is vital for our <u>water supply</u>.

* <u>Groundwater storage</u> occurs in <u>underground rocks</u> which are porous — they <u>collect water</u> in the pores, which are spaces between their particles.

* <u>Soil water storage</u> is when water is stored in the <u>soil</u> and is used by <u>plants</u>.

* <u>Short-term storage</u> occurs after interception on things like <u>plant leaves</u>.

Evaporated Water is the <u>Output</u>

There are <u>three</u> ways that water can get back into the atmosphere:
* <u>Evaporation</u> happens when sea, lake or river water is heated by the <u>Sun</u>. The water vapour <u>rises</u>, then <u>cools</u> and <u>condenses</u> to form <u>clouds</u>.

* <u>Transpiration</u> is when <u>plants</u> lose moisture.

* <u>Evapotranspiration</u> is both evaporation and transpiration together.

<u>P</u> Precipitation
<u>In</u> Interception
<u>Tr</u> Transpiration
<u>S</u> Surface run-off
<u>C</u> Channel flow
<u>E</u> Evaporation

<u>I</u> Infiltration
<u>T</u> Through flow
<u>Pe</u> Percolation
<u>G</u> Groundwater flow

The water cycle

Drainage Basins

Drainage basins are major components of the hydrosphere.
Each separate river system has its own drainage basin.

A River Basin has Several Important <u>Features</u>

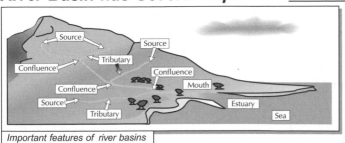

Important features of river basins

- The <u>source</u> is where a river <u>starts</u>, usually in an upland area.

- A <u>tributary</u> is a <u>stream</u> that joins the main river.

- A <u>confluence</u> is the point where two rivers join.

- The <u>mouth</u> is where the river flows into the sea.

- An <u>estuary</u> is where the mouth is <u>low enough</u> to let <u>sea enter</u> at high tide.
  This causes <u>deposition</u>, forming mud banks, which the river flows between.

A <u>Drainage Basin</u> is a Land Area Drained by a River

The terms <u>catchment area</u> and <u>drainage basin</u> mean the same thing — the <u>land area</u> from which a river and its tributaries <u>collect</u> the rainwater passing from the <u>soil</u> and <u>rock</u>. The land provides the <u>water</u> for the <u>main river</u> and its <u>tributaries</u>. The size of the catchment area depends on the size of the <u>river</u>.

A <u>watershed</u> is high ground <u>separating</u> two neighbouring drainage basins. On one side of the watershed the water drains in one direction, and on the other side it drains the opposite way.

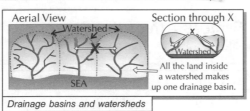

Drainage basins and watersheds

A Drainage Basin Works as a <u>System</u>

Water enters the drainage basin as <u>precipitation</u>. It goes through a series of <u>flows</u> and <u>stores</u> before reaching the sea as <u>river run-off</u>. The time between rain and river run-off depends on the <u>characteristics</u> of the basin — i.e. its shape, size, rock type and vegetation.

<u>Energy</u> is put into the system by the <u>steepness</u> of the hills / valley and the <u>force of gravity</u>. Water moves <u>rock</u> and <u>soil</u> material through the drainage basin system. It's <u>picked up</u> when the water energy is <u>high</u> and <u>deposited</u> when energy is <u>low</u>.

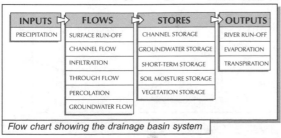

Flow chart showing the drainage basin system

The Storm Hydrograph

Hydrographs are used to study the flow of rivers
and predict when floods are likely.

The Storm _Hydrograph_ is Used for _Flood Prediction_

The graph shows the <u>change in river discharge</u> (volume of water flowing
per second) over a <u>short period</u> of time after a storm. It's used to work out
when a flood might be coming.

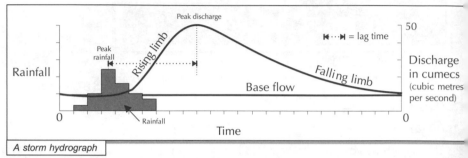

A storm hydrograph

- The <u>base flow</u> is the <u>normal discharge</u> of the river.
- The <u>rising limb</u> represents the <u>increase in discharge</u> after the storm.
- The <u>falling</u> or <u>recession limb</u> represents the <u>decrease in discharge</u>.
- The <u>lag time</u> is the <u>amount of time</u> between <u>peak rainfall</u> and <u>peak discharge</u>

The river is likely to flood when the graph is steep. This is because there is a
rapid increase in discharge over a short period of time — the river system is
unable to transport it away before it floods onto the surrounding land.

Several Factors Affect the _Steepness_ of the Graph

The <u>steeper</u> the graph, the <u>more likely</u> the river is to flood:

FACTOR	STEEPER	
1. Total Rainfall	High	
2. Intensity of Rain	High	(runs off)
3. Wetness of Ground	Saturated	(runs off)
4. Rock Type	Impermeable	(runs off)
5. Ground Cover	Bare Soil	(runs off)
6. Slope Angle	Steep	(runs quickly)

Factors which lead to a steeper storm hydrograph

FACTOR	GENTLER	
1. Total Rainfall	Low	
2. Intensity of Rain	Low	(soaks in)
3. Wetness of Ground	Dry	(soaks in)
4. Rock Type	Porous	(soaks in)
5. Ground Cover	Vegetated	(soaks in))
6. Slope Angle	Gentle	(runs slowly)

Factors which lead to a gentler storm hydrograph

Water Demand and Supply

Water supplies have to be <u>managed</u> to reduce the likelihood of shortages and to reduce pollution.

Water is <u>Stored</u> and <u>Transferred</u> Within and Between Countries

In Britain, the water supply is managed by the <u>water authorities</u>. The authorities <u>collect</u> and <u>distribute</u> water as well as <u>treating</u> and disposing of waste water.

<u>New reservoirs</u> have been built to increase storage. Water is also <u>transferred</u> to areas where there are shortages via <u>pipes</u>. In the EU water is transferred across <u>international boundaries</u>.

Water Demand is Growing all the time

Until recently, people in the <u>UK</u> have taken an adequate water supply for <u>granted</u>, but more <u>demand</u> and a series of drier than average years means <u>shortages</u>.

Rainfall is <u>heaviest</u> in the north and west, but there are more <u>people</u> and <u>industries</u> (so more water demand) in the drier south and east. Rain is also <u>heavier</u> in winter, but <u>demand</u> is <u>higher</u> in summer.

Supply doesn't meet demand, so people have to be <u>water conscious</u>. <u>Storage</u> and <u>movement</u> of water is necessary but <u>expensive,</u> and <u>quality</u> must be <u>controlled</u>.

Many <u>LEDCs</u> have Serious <u>Water Supply Problems</u>

In 1995, two billion people had <u>no clean water supply</u> — 40% of the world's population. This is a major <u>health hazard</u> which causes 80% of diseases in LEDCs. <u>Demand</u> for water is <u>increasing</u> as countries develop and populations grow, which worsens the problem. <u>Sanitation</u> (a proper sewage system) is also <u>limited</u> to 40% of the world's people. The rest do without.

Drought

<u>Rainfall supplies</u> can often be <u>unreliable</u> and <u>limited</u> in LEDCs — especially hot countries. In the worst cases, <u>droughts</u> can ruin crops and leave thousands without enough clean water. The <u>UN</u> estimates that by 2025, <u>two thirds</u> of the world's population won't have reliable, clean water.

LEDCs Can <u>Improve</u> the Water Situation

- Farmers can use <u>sprays</u> or 'drip-feeding' to water crops so no water is <u>wasted</u>.
- <u>Self-help schemes</u> can enable people to build <u>simple wells</u> like tube wells.
- <u>Concrete lining</u> of wells <u>reduces water loss</u> through evaporation and seepage.
- <u>Educating</u> people about <u>clean water</u> and <u>sanitation</u> is also important.

WORLD LOCATION

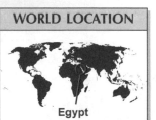
Egypt

Example: The Water Situation in <u>Egypt</u>

The <u>Aswan Dam</u> was built in the upper reaches of the <u>River Nile</u> in the 1960s to try to solve some of Egypt's water shortage problems. It has had both advantages and disadvantages.

ADVANTAGES	DISADVANTAGES
Steady water levels	More Bilharzia snails (cause serious disease in humans)
Flood control is possible	Less sediment washed onto flood plains — more fertiliser needed
Higher crop yields	Dam expensive to build
River navigable all year	Hot country — high water loss due to high evaporation rates
HEP schemes provide power to help economic development	Sediment will eventually fill reservoir

EGYPT LOCATION

Water Management

Rivers are _vital_ to people. So as well as learning about rivers themselves you need to understand the effects they have on people and how people use them.

Drainage Basins have _Many Uses_

- Farming: Lowland river valleys are good for farming — because of alluvium washed down in floods the soil is very _fertile_, and in higher areas they're the only _flat land_.
- Water consumption and use: The water can be used in the home, in industry and farming — upper reaches can be _reservoirs_ for water storage, and _dams_ can generate hydro-electric power (HEP).
- Transport: Most main rivers can be used for _moving goods_ or _people_.
- Settlement: Nearly all towns are built near a river for _historical reasons_, e.g. local water supply and transport.
- Recreation: Rivers are being used a lot more these days for _leisure activities_ like boating or fishing.
- Conservation: People nowadays are concerned about _wildlife_ and want to _conserve river habitats_.
- Afforestation: Many highland river slopes are being _planted_ with _trees_ to supply increasing demand for wood and paper.

There are _Different Opinions_ About _Water Management_

Different groups of people want different things and they all think they're right. But _anything done_ to the river affects everyone and can have _good_ or _bad effects_ on the river basin resources.

Examples	Good Consequences	Bad Consequences
Afforestation	More wood less soil erosion, less flooding	Lower river levels more deposition as lower velocity
Waste disposal	Using rivers saves money on processing	Polluted water downstream Raised temperatures disturb local ecology
Irrigation	Crops grow well in irrigated areas	Less water downstream
Dam-building	Controls water flow and floods lower down	Sediment free water let out — deltas shrink — no fertile silt lower down
Urbanisation	New houses etc. available	More artificial surfaces give more / quicker surface run-off and possibly flash floods

Water Authorities are _Private Companies_

The water supply companies in the UK are part of the _private sector_. That means that they are managed, amongst other things, to make a _profit_. People paying for the service through their water charges expect a _regular_ and _reliable_ service.

Many people ask if profit-making companies are doing all they can to maintain supplies effectively. Many would favour a system of national, _centralised_ management with _tighter controls_ and _more investment_.

The water authorities are regulated by the _Environment Agency_ (EA) in England and Wales and by the _Scottish Environment Protection Agency_ (SEPA) in Scotland. The EA makes sure the water authorities are doing things safely and sustainably.

Flooding in MEDCs and LEDCs

Floods nearly always have negative consequences, but the effects are generally <u>worse</u> in <u>LEDCs</u>.

There are <u>Human</u> and <u>Physical Causes</u> of Flooding

The causes of flooding are a combination of the effects of <u>nature</u> and <u>human activity</u>:

Human causes of flooding	Natural causes of flooding
Deforestation	Heavy rainfall
Draining floodplains	Rapid melting of snow
Urbanisation (impermeable surfaces increase run-off)	Frozen ground allowing rapid run-off

An *MEDC* <u>*Flood Example*</u> — *Lynmouth, Devon 1952*

There was <u>no early warning system</u> in spite of known <u>high peak discharges</u>, so the signs of an imminent flood went unnoticed.

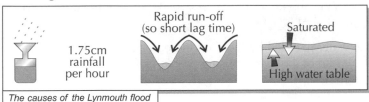

1.75cm rainfall per hour

Rapid run-off (so short lag time)

Saturated

High water table

The causes of the Lynmouth flood

Lynmouth

Other factors made the flood <u>worse</u>:

- <u>Blocked bridges</u> made <u>temporary dams</u> which later <u>burst</u> causing a <u>12 metre high wave</u> to move downstream at 30 km/h.

- Near the mouth, the river had been <u>channelled</u> into a <u>culvert</u> in the town, making a <u>narrow outlet</u> to the sea. This man-made channel <u>couldn't cope</u> with the <u>extra discharge</u> so the river <u>changed direction</u> and made its own exit to the sea.

The resulting flood caused <u>casualties</u> and <u>damage</u>:

- 34 <u>dead</u>
- 1000 <u>homeless</u>
- 90 buildings <u>destroyed</u>
- 150 cars/boats <u>lost</u>

In an <u>LEDC</u> like <u>Bangladesh</u> Floods are <u>Even Worse</u>

Some <u>LEDCs</u> use river flooding to cover farmland with <u>fertile alluvium</u> and to provide water for <u>irrigation channels</u> — e.g. the Ganges Valley and Bangladesh delta. However, flood disasters can cause serious damage in LEDCs because their flood <u>preparation</u>, <u>defence</u> and <u>recovery</u> are all lacking, compared to MEDCs.

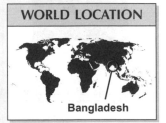

Bangladesh

- <u>Severe floods</u> can destroy food supplies, homes, etc. <u>Emergency services</u> and <u>money</u> are <u>limited</u> in LEDCs, making recovery <u>more difficult</u>.

- In <u>1988 Bangladesh</u> experienced its worst floods in living memory. 7 million homes were destroyed and over 2000 people were <u>killed</u>.

- Floods are often completely <u>unexpected</u>. They usually happen in <u>flatter</u>, <u>lower-lying</u> valleys which are <u>built up</u> and <u>heavily populated</u>.

India

Bangladesh

Bay of Bengal

Flood Control – Hard Engineering

Hard engineering involves building structures like dams to <u>control</u> the river syste

Dams can Control Discharge for a Valley

<u>Dams</u> and <u>reservoirs</u> in the <u>upper</u> parts of a drainage basin are very effective for <u>controlling</u> the <u>discharge</u> lower down the valley — where the flood threat is greatest. Dams are <u>expensive</u> to build so recently <u>multi-purpose</u> schemes have been built, including <u>hydro-electric power</u> (HEP) stations and <u>recreational lakes</u> — e.g. at Kielder in Northumberland.

HEP provided if required →

Reduces / controls river discharge lower down

Recreation / leisure uses possible

The uses of dams

The <u>disadvantage</u> of such schemes is that beautiful <u>countryside</u> can be <u>spoiled</u> b ugly buildings. Also, <u>farmland</u> is <u>destroyed</u> when upper valley floors are flooded

All the river <u>sediment</u> is deposited in the reservoir instead of on the floodplain downstream. This means the floodplain is <u>less fertile</u>, forcing the farmers to use more fertiliser. Also <u>coastal beaches</u> and <u>deltas</u> lose their sediment.

The sediment-free water released by the dam <u>increases erosion</u> downstream. This increases the width of the river, causing problems for bridges and buildings near the river.

The River's Shape can be Changed to Control Flooding

<u>Increasing</u> the capacity of the channel means it can hold more water in a flood.

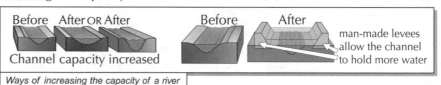

Before After OR After

Channel capacity increased

Before   After

man-made levees allow the channel to hold more water

Ways of increasing the capacity of a river

<u>Culverts</u> straighten and line the river channel to increase the speed of the river and remove excess water more quickly down the channel to the sea.

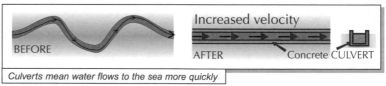

BEFORE

Increased velocity

AFTER   Concrete CULVERT

Culverts mean water flows to the sea more quickly

Building <u>branching channels</u> off the main river can remove excess water in <u>three</u> ways:

• Taking water to a <u>neighbouring basin</u> with a cut-through.

• Diverting extra water into <u>storage areas</u> on the flood plain.

• Building <u>relief channels</u> around towns to hold the excess water.

Artificial Changes to River Channels can Cause Problems

• Channels need regular <u>dredging</u> to stop the channel size decreasing.

• Increased channel speed causes flooding and erosion <u>downstream</u>.

• The engineering often looks <u>ugly</u> and affects the natural river <u>ecosystems</u>.

• If a dam, levee or cut-through breaks there could be a <u>big</u>, <u>sudden</u> disaster.

Flood Control – Soft Engineering

To avoid the disadvantages of hard engineering, water authorities are moving to more sustainable flood controls, using 'soft engineering'. Instead of trying to control rivers, soft engineering works by using natural drainage basin processes to reduce flooding.

Prediction — Spotting Problems Before they Happen

Soft engineering relies on detailed research into drainage basin systems to work out how to solve one flood problem without causing new ones. To find out if an area is in danger of flooding, the whole drainage basin is looked at. Scientists assess the geology, soil, drainage and precipitation characteristics of the drainage basin.

They also investigate the human activities in the basin to make sure they've got a good overview of all the factors which affect channel flow in the basin. Another way of finding out when floods are likely to happen is to look for patterns in the flood-history data for the river.

EXAM TIP

Remember soft engineering is really popular in geography at the moment because it is more sustainable than hard engineering. It's worth learning because it comes up in the coasts section too (see page 37).

Changing Land Use can help Reduce Flooding

One of the easiest 'soft engineering' ways of avoiding flood problems is not to build houses where it floods. But many people already live in flood zones and they're not leaving, so different strategies are needed.

Afforestation of bare slopes in the upper reaches reduces run-off as trees intercept the rain. Lag time is longer, with less run-off or river discharge.

Leaving land up river as pasture gives a continuous plant cover, reducing run-off water which the plants intercept. It's better than arable crops, where the soil is bare during the non-growing season.

Man-made surfaces, such as concrete, allow rapid run-off, which encourages flooding. Plants and grass areas can be used instead to reduce this problem.

Traditional man-made drainage systems use fast draining pipes leading directly into watercourses causing floods.

| Afforestation |
| Pasture land |
| Plants and grass areas in towns |
| Sustainable Urban Drainage Systems (SUDS) |

Soft engineering methods

This problem is solved by Sustainable Urban Drainage Systems (SUDS) which reduce the flow and amount of urban drainage by directing rainwater into the soil, slow draining channels or ponds.

TIP

LEDCs are lagging behind — soft engineering is predominantly used in MEDCs where there's more money available to invest in flood prediction, prevention and control.

Things Aren't Getting any Better

Scientists believe that the severe flooding we've had in recent years could be an effect of global warming. If this is true, flood control will be even more important in the future.

Flooding could become more common

TIP

See page 17 for more about global warming.

27

Water Shortage

Water shortage leads to two massive problems which affect millions of people across the world — <u>drought</u> and <u>desertification</u>.

Drought — *When <u>Rainfall</u> Doesn't Meet People's Needs*

Drought doesn't just mean low rainfall — in some parts of the world there is always low rainfall and the people adjust accordingly.

Drought occurs when <u>much less</u> rain falls than would normally be expected.

Drought Affects <u>MEDCs</u> and <u>LEDCs</u> Differently

In MEDCs low rainfall means that water supplies drop. <u>Reservoirs</u> are rarely full, <u>river flows</u> are down and <u>ground water</u> levels fall steadily. Whilst the amount of water <u>available</u> in the UK has decreased, <u>demand</u> from industry and the public has increased (see page 23).

Drought can be devastating to agriculture, as lack of water for <u>irrigation</u> causes <u>crop failure</u>. This leads to loss of income and, in LEDCs that rely on subsistence farming, it causes malnutrition and starvation. In extreme cases, <u>famine</u> occurs — starvation on a massive scale.

In some LEDCs, like <u>Belize</u>, water shortages are worsened by hotels catering for <u>tourists</u> from MEDCs. They use lots of water to meet the demands of their guests.

MEDCs can cope well with drought because they have better water <u>storage facilities</u> and people don't rely on <u>subsistence crops</u>. Drought is far worse in LEDCs. Often the only way for people to survive is to accept <u>foreign aid</u>.

<u>Desertification</u> Starts Through a <u>Shortage</u> of Water

Desertification is where <u>grasslands</u> are turned into <u>desert</u>. The <u>Sahel</u> region in Africa has turned from savanna to desert and scrub. <u>Long-term drought</u> is the main cause of <u>desertification</u> but the effects are made worse by <u>people</u>.

<u>Soil erosion</u> is gradually turning the land to desert.

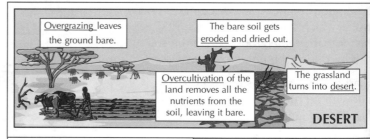

Desertification of the savanna grassland

There are <u>three</u> ways in which people contribute to desertification:

- <u>Increased population</u> means <u>more trees</u> are cut down for fuel, and <u>larger herds</u> overgraze the land — vegetation is removed and the ground is left bare, causing <u>soil erosion</u>.

- <u>Climate fluctuations</u> — several years of adequate rainfall encourages farmers to <u>enlarge herds</u> and <u>grow crops</u>. If dry years follow, the land <u>can't support</u> increased herds and <u>soil erosion</u> occurs.

- <u>Commercial agriculture</u> uses <u>valuable water</u> and pushes subsistence farmers onto marginal land that cannot support farming.

Methods like <u>terracing</u>, planting <u>hedges</u> and farming in a <u>less intensive</u> way can help to prevent desertification in areas which are at risk.

Recently scientists have discovered that desertification isn't always permanent. If the land is carefully <u>managed</u> it can slowly <u>recover</u> and vegetation can <u>regrow</u>.

EXAMPLE

Effects of drought in Ethiopia, 1983-84:

- **500 000 people died, mostly of starvation**
- **many people migrated from remote areas to refugee camps in Sudan**
- **Ethiopia is still reliant on aid from foreign governments and charities**

EXAMPLE

This map shows the extent of severe desertification in Africa:

☐ Area of severe desertification

1 Niger   4 Ethiopia
2 Chad   5 Somalia
3 Sudan

EXAM TIP

It's worth mentioning in your exam answer that solving the major problems of civil wars and overpopulation would help prevent desertification a huge amount — but these are very hard to deal with.

Case Studies

You need to learn these case studies about flooding in an MEDC and an LEDC.

Case Study 1: _The Northampton Flood of Easter, 1998_

<u>Between 9th-12th April 1998</u>, heavy rain fell in the UK, causing widespread <u>flooding</u>. <u>Northampton</u> was seriously flooded when the <u>River Nene</u> burst its banks. A number of <u>characteristics</u> mean the Nene is likely to flood in Northampton:

- The <u>valleys</u> of the upper catchment are <u>steep and narrow</u> so they channel water swiftly towards the main river.

- The <u>impermeable clay</u> which underlies most of the area prevents water from draining away.

- The <u>Pitsford reservoir</u> and the <u>Grand Union Canal</u> overflow into the Nene if they reach maximum capacity.

- The <u>floodplain</u> has been <u>heavily built on</u> in Northampton.

- The <u>confluence</u> of the Nene and the Brampton tributary is in Northampton.

UK LOCATION

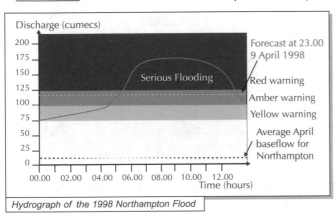

Hydrograph of the 1998 Northampton Flood

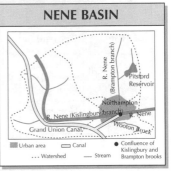

NENE BASIN

The <u>hydrograph</u> shows that the river flow was much higher than had been predicted. The river rose very rapidly and <u>broke its banks at 04.00hrs</u>. It reached <u>170 cumecs</u> at dawn.

There was <u>no evacuation</u> or warnings because the flood was not expected to be so serious. There was a huge amount of <u>damage</u> to <u>property</u> and <u>infrastructure</u>.

Case Study 2: _Flooding in Mozambique, 2000_

In <u>February and March 2000</u>, the heaviest rain for 50 years hit many countries in southern Africa. In February 1163 mm of rain fell — the average for February is 177 mm.

- Most of the rivers in South West Africa drain east to the Mozambique coast, where they enter the Indian Ocean. Mozambique suffered the worst floods.

- At the same time, Cyclone Eline struck Mozambique and increased the amount of floodwater.

- In Mozambique over 1000 people were drowned and millions more were made homeless.

- The only way to rescue people from the floods was either by air or by boat. Helicopters and rubber dinghies were needed quickly as well as aircraft to drop food and medical supplies.

A poor LEDC like Mozambique has very limited resources so they relied on aid sent from MEDCs. A media campaign which showed images of people stranded in Mozambique was used to raise aid in MEDCs like Britain.

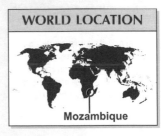

WORLD LOCATION

Mozambique

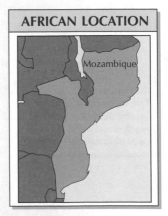

AFRICAN LOCATION

Erosion, Transportation & Deposition

The ways that a river shapes the landscape can be grouped into three categories
— erosion (removing), transportation (moving) and deposition (leaving behind).

Erosion is When the River Wears Land Away

Rivers erode in four main ways, called <u>erosion processes</u>:

- <u>Corrasion</u> or <u>abrasion</u> is when large pieces of bedload material <u>wear away</u> the riverbed and banks — e.g. in floods.

- <u>Attrition</u> means the rocks being transported are <u>eroded</u>. The sediment particles knock against the bed or each other and break apart.

- <u>Hydraulic action</u> is when the <u>force of the water</u> wears away at <u>softer rocks</u>.

- <u>Solution</u> or <u>corrosion</u> is when chalk and limestone <u>dissolve</u> in water.

River Erosion is Headward, Vertical or Lateral

<u>Headward erosion</u> is when the furthest point upstream, the <u>valley head</u>, is worn away by <u>rainwash</u>, <u>undercutting</u> (see page 31) or <u>soil creep</u> (the slow movement of soil downhill over time).

<u>Vertical erosion</u> deepens the valley as the <u>water force grows</u> — common in the <u>upper stage</u> when the gradient is steep.

<u>Lateral erosion</u> widens the valley, combined with <u>weathering</u> of the sides — it's common in <u>middle</u> and <u>lower</u> stage valleys.

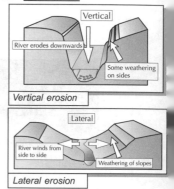

Vertical erosion

Lateral erosion

Transportation is the Movement of Eroded Material

A river transports its load downstream in four ways:

- <u>Suspension</u> is when fine silt and clay material is <u>carried</u> along in the water.

- <u>Saltation</u> is when small sand-sized particles are <u>bounced</u> along the <u>riverbed</u>.

- <u>Traction</u> is when <u>larger</u> materials like boulders are <u>dragged</u> along the bed.

- <u>Solution</u> is when eroded material <u>dissolved</u> in the water is <u>carried away</u>.

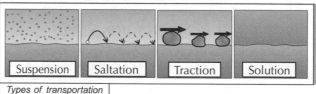

| Suspension | Saltation | Traction | Solution |

Types of transportation

Deposition is When a River Dumps its Load

It can happen when the <u>velocity</u> is <u>lower</u> than normal and the river can't move as much material. It also happens when a river's <u>load</u> is <u>increased</u> — e.g. after a landslide. <u>Deposition</u> can form <u>deltas</u> where rivers enter a <u>sea</u> or <u>lake</u>.

There are <u>four stages</u> of deposition:

- <u>Large material</u> carried by the river is <u>deposited</u> in the <u>higher reaches</u>.

- <u>Gravel, sand and silt</u> carried as bedload or in suspension are laid down in the <u>lower reaches</u>.

- Fine particles of <u>suspended silt</u> and <u>clay</u> are laid down in <u>estuaries</u> and <u>deltas</u>.

- <u>Dissolved load</u> is <u>not</u> deposited, but stays in solution and is carried out to sea.

River Features of the Upper Stage

Many of the more notable and dramatic river features are found at the upper stage.

Interlocking Spurs are Caused by Erosion

In its upper stage the river erodes vertically rather than laterally.

Interlocking spurs are ridges produced when a river in the upper stage twists and turns round obstacles of hard rock along its downward pathway.

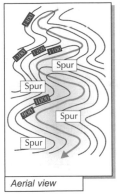

Aerial view

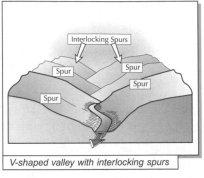

V-shaped valley with interlocking spurs

These ridges interlock with one another like the teeth of a zip fastener.

EXAMPLE
Interlocking spurs are found in the upper stages of many British rivers, such as the River Ouse in Yorkshire.

Waterfalls are Found at Steep Parts of the River Bed

A layer of hard rock won't erode very easily so when the river reaches it, any softer rocks on the downstream side are eroded more quickly. This means the river bed gets steeper where it crosses the hard rocks and a waterfall forms.

Waterfalls can form when the hard rock is horizontal, vertical or dips upstream (rock slopes down as you go upstream). At the foot of the waterfall the water wears away the softer rock to form a plunge pool.

As the waterfall retreats and eats its way upstream, a recessional gorge is formed.

EXAMPLE
Niagara Falls, on the American-Canadian border

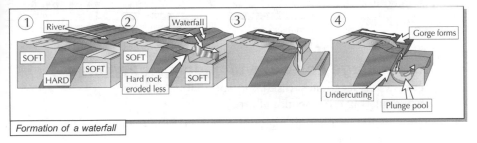

Formation of a waterfall

Rapids are a Series of Little Waterfalls

Rapids are found where there are alternate bands of hard and soft rock:

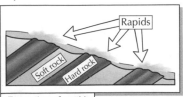

Formation of rapids

They can also be found when a hard rock layer dips downstream:

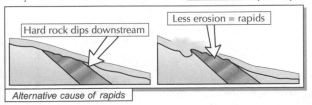

Alternative cause of rapids

EXAMPLE
The Colorado Rapids (USA)

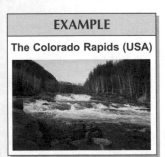

31

River Features of Middle & Lower Stage

Middle and lower stage river features are often more temporary and changeable than upper stage features.

The Middle and Lower Stages have *Meanders*

The river now has a <u>large discharge</u>, <u>gentle gradient</u> and <u>lateral erosion</u>. It develops a more winding pathway with <u>large bends</u> — these bends are called <u>meanders</u>.

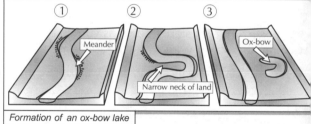

Formation of meanders

The river twists — over time the course of the meander migrates <u>downstream</u>. The current is <u>fastest</u> on the <u>outside</u> of the meander curve because the river channel is <u>deeper</u> there — on the <u>inside</u> it's <u>shallow</u> so the current is <u>slower</u>.

<u>River cliffs</u> are found on the meander's <u>outer edge</u> where the river causes more erosion. <u>Point bars</u> are on the <u>inner edge</u> where sandy material is <u>deposited</u> by the slower-moving river — above river level they're <u>slip-off slopes</u>.

Ox-Bow Lakes are Formed from Wide Meander Loops

<u>Meander loops</u> can become so <u>sinuous</u> (wavy) that the river's easiest path is <u>straight across</u>, so it breaks through the narrow <u>neck of land</u> in between.

The <u>outer part</u> of the loop is left <u>isolated</u> from the river as an <u>ox-bow lake</u>.

Formation of an ox-bow lake

The Lower Stage has Several Important Features

The river now has its greatest discharge and mass — it has a really big cross-sectional area.

- <u>Alluvium</u> is the term for <u>all material</u> deposited by a river. It's usually very <u>fertile</u>.

- The <u>flood plain</u> is the <u>wide valley floor</u> which the river regularly floods. It's <u>flat</u> and covered by alluvium, making it <u>good farmland</u>.

- <u>Levees</u> are <u>raised river banks</u>, made of coarse river load material deposited during <u>floods</u>.

- <u>Estuaries</u> are <u>funnel-shaped river mouths</u>. Most are found where an existing river has had its lower reaches flooded after changes in <u>sea level</u>.

- <u>Deltas</u> form when a river deposits silt <u>too fast</u> for the sea to remove it. There are three main types:

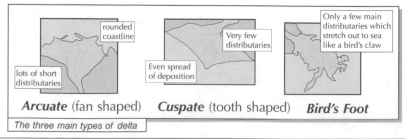

Arcuate (fan shaped)   **Cuspate** (tooth shaped)   **Bird's Foot**

The three main types of delta

Case Studies

You need to know a case study of the features of a particular river system.

Case Study: The <u>Usk Basin</u> in <u>South Wales</u>

The River Usk in <u>South Wales</u> runs from its source in the <u>Brecon Beacons</u> to its mouth at <u>Newport</u> on the <u>Bristol Channel</u>. The nature of the river catchment area changes as the river flows from the uplands to the coastal lowlands. Processes of <u>erosion</u>, <u>transport</u> and <u>deposition</u> are evident throughout its course. When the speed of the water <u>increases</u>, then the processes of <u>corrosion</u>, <u>attrition</u> and <u>hydraulic action</u> dominate. When the speed of the water <u>decreases</u>, deposition occurs.

UK LOCATION

Usk Basin

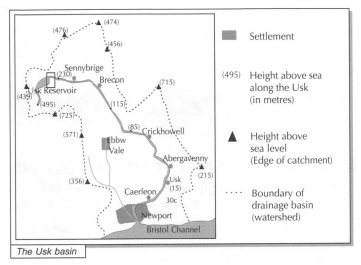

The Usk basin

The <u>characteristics</u> of the River Usk differ between its <u>source</u> and its <u>mouth</u>.

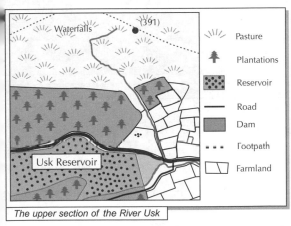

The upper section of the River Usk

At its source the Usk follows a very <u>steep gradient</u> off the fellside. The <u>vertical erosion</u> of the river has formed <u>interlocking spurs</u> on the pasture land. There are also some <u>waterfalls</u> on the pasture, where the river flows over bands of hard rock. There are <u>no meanders</u> and <u>no flood plain</u> on the upper section of the river. Some of the water drains into the Usk reservoir.

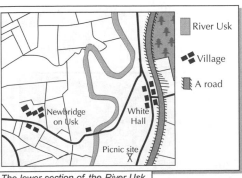

The lower section of the River Usk

Near its mouth the <u>gradient</u> of the river Usk is very <u>gentle</u> and it flows less rapidly than in the upper section. There are <u>no waterfalls or interlocking spurs</u>. Here the river has a <u>large floodplain</u> and lots of <u>big meanders</u>. Two towns, White Hall and Newbridge on Usk, are located near meanders, although the river's course has shifted since the original settlement.

Coastal Landforms from Erosion

Wave erosion forms many coastal features over long periods of time.

Rock Erosion Forms Cliffs

Waves erode rocks along the shoreline by hydraulic action, corrosion, corrasion and pounding. A notch is slowly formed at the high water mark which may develop into a cave. Rock above the notch becomes unstable with nothing to support it, and it collapses.

The coastline can retreat over many years as this process continues to form a wave cut platform with cliffs behind. The actual size and angle of the cliff will depend on the local rock and its hardness, etc.

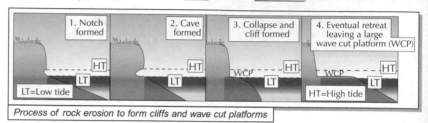

Process of rock erosion to form cliffs and wave cut platforms

Eroded Hard and Soft Rocks form Headlands

If there are alternate bands of hard and softer rock in the coastline, the harder rocks take longer to erode than the softer rocks — because the sea has less effe[ct]

The hard rock will be left jutting out forming one or more headlands — usually with cliffs. The softer rock will be eroded to form bays — the erosion means tha[t] the bays will usually slope more gently inland, creating room for a beach to for[m.]

Again, the local geology will affect the actual shape and size of the features formed.

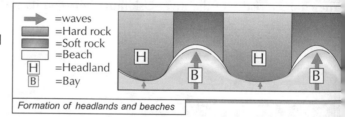

Formation of headlands and beaches

Caves, Arches and Stacks can also be Formed

A crack or rock weakness in a headland can be eroded — wave energy is usuall[y] strong there because the headland juts out. This forms one or more caves.

Occasionally the pressure of air, compressed in the caves by the waves, weaken[s] the roof along a major joint and the rock collapses to form a blow hole. Further erosion enlarges the cave and it breaks through the headland, forming an arch.

The roof of this arch is often unstable and eventually collapses leaving a stack or series of stacks.

Areas with a limestone or chalk geology are prone to this kind of erosion.

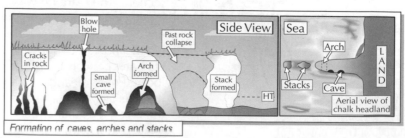

Formation of caves, arches and stacks

Coastal Landforms from Deposition

Deposition forms specific coastal features.

Beaches are formed by _Deposition_

Beaches are found on coastlines where eroded material in the sea has been deposited — e.g. in bays between headlands. They vary in size from tiny inlets to vast stretches. Beach fragment size depends on local rock type and wave energy.

Storm beaches are ridges of boulders at the landward side of beaches. They are caused by heavy seas piling up material at the high-tide mark.

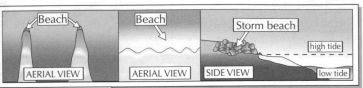
Different types of beach

Spits are Long Beaches formed by _Longshore Drift_

Spits are sand or pebble beaches sticking out to sea, but joined to the land at one end — they are mainly formed by longshore drift. Spits tend form across river mouths, where the coast suddenly changes direction, or where tides meet calmer waters of a bay or inlet. At the spit end there are usually some hooks or recurves formed by occasional strong winds from another direction. Waves can't reach the sea areas behind the spit, so they're often mud flats and salt marshes.

Formation of a mature spit

KEY TERM

Longshore drift is the sideways movement of material along the coast in a zig zag pattern, due to angled waves.

Tombolos and _Barrier Beaches_ Join Land Together

Tombolos are found where an island is joined to the mainland by a ridge of deposited material, e.g. Chesil Beach on the south coast of England — this is 18km long and joins the Isle of Portland to the mainland.

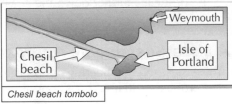
Chesil beach tombolo

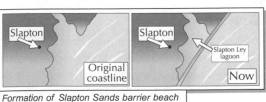
Formation of Slapton Sands barrier beach

Barrier beaches are found where a spit extends right across a shallow bay, e.g. Slapton Sands in south Devon — the water behind it is left as a lagoon.

Waves _Transport_ Material in _Four Ways_

Eroded material is transported by waves, eroded further and deposited further along the coast. It is transported in the same ways as a river transports its load:

- Suspension — fine sand is carried along in the water itself.
- Saltation — small pebbles and boulders are bounced along the sea bed.
- Traction — larger pebbles and boulders are dragged along the sea bed.
- Solution — eroded material is carried dissolved in the water.

EXAMPLES

Fine sand beach

Blackpool

Pebble beach

Hastings

Spits

Mouth of River Exe, Devon

Orford Ness, Suffolk

Tombolo

Chesil beach, south coast of England

Barrier beach

Slapton Sands, S. Devon

Managing Coasts

There are two different approaches to defending against coastal erosion and flooding — <u>hard</u> and <u>soft</u> engineering.

There are <u>Five</u> main <u>Hard Engineering</u> Defences

- <u>Groynes</u> are wooden structures placed at right angles to the coast where longshore drift occurs. They <u>reduce</u> movement of material along the coast, and <u>hold</u> the beach in place — <u>protecting</u> the cliff from further erosion in some parts. The beach will then <u>protect</u> low areas from <u>flooding</u>.

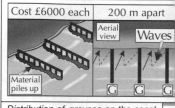

Cost £6000 each   200 m apart

Aerial view   Waves

Material piles up

Distribution of groynes on the coast

Cost £2000 per metre

sea wall   sea

Sea wall

- <u>Sea walls</u> reduce erosion — but they <u>deflect</u> (not absorb) waves so waves can still <u>wash away</u> the protective beach. The waves also <u>erode</u> the wall itself which can collapse. Sea walls <u>protect</u> against <u>floods</u> in lowland coasts.

- <u>Revetments</u> (slatted barriers) are built where a sea wall would be <u>too expensive</u>, e.g. out of towns. They <u>break</u> the wave force, trapping beach material behind them and <u>protecting</u> the cliff base — they're <u>cheaper</u> than sea walls but look unattractive and <u>don't</u> give full protection.

- <u>Gabions</u> are steel mesh cages containing boulders, built onto the cliff face above a sea wall. The rocks <u>absorb</u> some of the wave energy and <u>cut down</u> erosion — they're cheap but ugly.

- <u>Armour blocks</u> are large boulders piled on beaches where erosion is likely. They're cheap but ugly and they can be <u>undermined</u> or <u>moved by waves</u>.

These <u>hard engineering</u> style sea defences are <u>not sustainable</u> in the long term. They are extremely <u>expensive</u>, <u>ugly</u>, need constant <u>maintenance</u> and often cause <u>problems</u> further down the coast.

A More <u>Sustainable</u> Approach — <u>Soft Engineering</u>

The easiest <u>soft engineering</u> option is to leave the sea to do what it wants. The problem is that without control, the sea would <u>destroy</u> a lot of land by <u>floods</u> and <u>erosion</u>. Soft engineering approaches try to fit in with <u>natural</u> coastal processes and <u>protect habitats</u>.

- <u>Beach nourishment</u> — This simply means putting more mud or sand on the beach. The beach is an excellent natural flood defence, so by replacing all the sediment that's eroded, you avoid a big flood problem. The problem is how to get the sediment without causing <u>environmental damage</u> somewhere else. It's also pretty <u>expensive</u> and needs to be done again and again.

- <u>Shoreline vegetation</u> — Planting things like <u>marshbeds</u> on the shoreline <u>binds</u> the beach sediment together, slowing erosion. This also encourages shoreline <u>habitats</u> to develop.

- <u>Dune stabilisation</u> — Dunes are an excellent defence against <u>storm floods</u>. Sediment is added and erosion is <u>reduced</u> by footpath control and <u>marram grass</u> planting. This supports the dune ecosystem.

Dunes are good sea defence

- <u>Set backs</u> — Building houses set back from the coast.

EXAMPLES

Groynes

Bournemouth

Sea wall

Scarborough

Armour blocks

Barton-on-Sea

KEY TERM

Soft engineering strategies aim to achieve <u>managed retreat</u> — this is about slowing coastal erosion but not trying to stop it. Eventually buildings will have to be moved or lost to the sea, but this can often be cheaper than investing in constant coastal control.

Humans and Natural Landforms

Human activities affect river and coastal landforms by altering the way that natural systems operate.

Human Activities *Have Effects on* Coastlines

Many human activities have effects on the coastlines. Some (like beach nourishment) are <u>deliberate</u> whilst others are just <u>caused by carelessness</u>.

The two most common human influences on coastlines are:

* <u>Deliberate hard and soft engineering strategies</u> (look back to page 36 for more detail on what these are). Hard strategies try to solve coastal problems in a specific place, but they usually impact on other places further along the coast. Soft engineering strategies attempt to fit in more with natural coastal processes, but both hard and soft engineering will always alter natural processes to a certain degree.

* <u>Accidental damage of beach ecosystems</u>. For example tourists often trample sand dunes to get to a beach. Also, water pollution from things like industrial waste, oil spills and sewage systems can damage marine ecosystems.

TIP
There's more about hard and soft engineering on page 36.

Coastal Protection *is a Priority*

Coastal areas need to be <u>managed</u> carefully either by <u>national bodies</u> such as the National Parks Authorities and the National Trust or by <u>local authorities</u>. Many coastlines are beautiful so lots of people visit them — but they're <u>fragile</u>.

Management strategies can minimise the damage caused by tourists, for example authorised <u>car parks</u> and <u>picnic sites</u>, well-marked footpaths and information leaflets about erosion. Footpaths can be <u>reinforced</u> and the areas at risk <u>fenced off</u> from the public.

Fragile sand dunes

People Affect Rivers *Too*

Just like coasts, many human activities have effects on drainage basins and rivers. Again, some (like building dams) are <u>deliberate</u> whilst others (like pollution) are just <u>consequences of other activities</u>.

Some of the most common human influences on drainage basins and river channels are:

* <u>Deliberate hard and soft engineering strategies</u>. Look back to pages 26 and 27 for more on this.

* <u>Water pollution</u> from things like farm land and industrial effluent pipes change river ecosystems. For example, the chemicals from farmers' fertilisers can drain into rivers and kill the plants and animals there.

* <u>Accidental damage</u> of river ecosystems. The recreational use of rivers can ruin natural habitats for plants and animals — for example by over-fishing, sailing in waterways like the Norfolk Broads or swimming in rivers like the River Dart in Dartmoor, Devon. Also, human use of rivers for practical purposes like irrigation and drinking water can disrupt natural river ecosystems.

EXAMPLE
The river Colorado in the American West is one of the longest rivers in the world. People use the water for drinking and for irrigation. The flow of the river has been changed so much that, apart from during floods, no water has reached the river's mouth at the Gulf of California for the last 30 years.

Management and Conflict

Different people have different ideas about how best to manage a coast or river

There are <u>Different Interest Groups</u>

Coastal and river protection is <u>expensive</u>. It's impossible to protect everything.

- <u>Residents</u> want to <u>preserve</u> their homes and livelihoods.

- <u>Tourists</u> want <u>access</u> to the areas without restriction.

- <u>Conservationists</u> want to <u>preserve local habitats</u> and <u>protect</u> rare wildlife.

- The <u>government</u> has to consider the effect of an action in one place on other places nearby, and also to use public money in the <u>best</u> possible way, benefiting the most people.

- Local authorities have to <u>look after</u> the <u>interests</u> of as many local people as possible in the most economical and satisfactory way.

Example: Should the <u>Holderness Coast</u> be <u>Protected</u>?

The Holderness coast is mainly made up of low cliffs made of <u>boulder clay</u>. This material was deposited 10 000 years ago at the end of the last ice age. It is a crumbly rock with <u>little resistance</u> to erosion from the sea.

Holderness
Coast

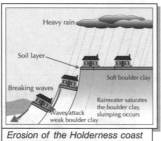

Erosion of the Holderness coast

In addition, the rock can become dangerously <u>saturated</u> with rainwater. It struggles to support its own weight and slumps into the sea.

In some places, the land is disappearing at a rate of <u>0.5 metres per year</u>.

What could be done to protect the coast?

The diagram on the right shows all the different methods that could be used to <u>reduce erosion</u> on the Holderness coast.

Defending the whole coast would be too <u>expensive</u> so the authorities have to choose which areas need protecting — inevitably this leads to <u>conflict</u>.

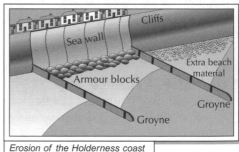

Erosion of the Holderness coast

FACT

**The Holderness coast has changed significantly over the last 10 000 years.
The yellow line on this map shows what the coastline will probably look like in 2100 AD if erosion continues at the current rate.**

There are many different ideas:

As the table below shows, there is a lot of conflict over managing the coastline.

Person	Opinion
Lynne, Withernsea resident	"Withernsea is a popular place for retirement — people wouldn't come here if they thought the sea was going to erode the sea front. I think maintaining the sea wall here should be a priority".
Toni, Cowden resident	"The erosion here has rapidly increased since protection was introduced in Mappleton. I think it's unfair that some areas get priority over others".
Tom, Spokesman, Easington Gas Terminal	"Our terminal at Easington is where North Sea gas comes ashore. The cliffs have retreated loads since the scheme was introduced at Mappleton. Some of the villagers at Easington are worried that the government will focus on protecting the terminal and they will suffer as a consequence. It's going to be a tough decision — whatever happens there will always be winners and losers."
Matt, Planning Officer, Local Council	"I've received a lot of interesting letters about coastal protection on Holderness. The trouble is that I've only got a limited budget to spend on protection — there's simply no way we can please everyone. We're trying to prioritise but it's not an easy task and the effort we make isn't always appreciated."

Case Studies

You need to know specific examples of coastal and river landforms.

Case Study 1: <u>*Dorset Coast — an Erosional Landscape*</u>

The Dorset coast is made from bands of <u>hard rock</u> (like Portland Stone and chalk) and <u>soft rock</u> (like Bagshot Beds and Weldon Sands), which have eroded at different rates giving a series of <u>headlands</u> (like Old Harry's Rocks) and <u>bays</u> (like Swanage Bay and Lulworth Cove). The <u>beautiful scenery</u> created by the erosion is popular with <u>tourists</u>.

UK LOCATION

Dorset Coast

The hard, rocky headlands are attacked by the waves. <u>Cracks</u> and <u>joints</u> have been opened up by waves to form caves, some of which have developed into <u>arches</u>, like the impressive Durdle Door. <u>Stacks</u> develop where arches collapse.

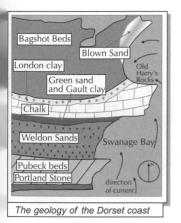

The geology of the Dorset coast

The arch, Durdle Door, in Dorset

Case Study 2: <u>*Spurn Head, Holderness coast*</u>

Spurn head is a <u>spit</u> which sticks out into the <u>Humber estuary</u> at the southern point of the Holderness coastline (see map on page 38). The spit has formed from material that is moved south along the coast by <u>longshore drift</u>.

The activities of people affect the spit in several different ways:

- The spit is a popular <u>tourist attraction</u>.

- There is a marsh behind the spit which is a protected <u>nature reserve</u>.

- The Humber estuary has to be <u>dredged</u> so that large boats can get to the <u>ports</u> of Hull and Grimsby.

- The use of <u>coastal protection</u> schemes like <u>groynes</u> further up the coast (for example at Mappleton) mean that the amount of material reaching the spit is reduced. This makes the spit more prone to <u>erosion</u>.

UK LOCATION

Spurn Head

Case Study 3: <u>*The Nile Delta, Egypt*</u>

The Nile is the longest river in the world. It flows through much of <u>Africa</u> and eventually flows out into the Mediterranean Sea in <u>Egypt</u>. The Nile carries a massive amount of <u>sediment</u>. Some of the sediment is deposited on <u>flood plains</u>. The rest forms a large <u>arcuate delta</u> at the mouth of the river.

People interact with the Nile delta in <u>three</u> main ways:

- The <u>flood plain</u> around the delta is <u>intensively farmed</u> because the soil is extremely <u>fertile</u>.

- Building <u>dams</u> upstream (like the Aswan) mean the <u>sediment flow</u> to the delta has been reduced.

- Severe <u>floods</u> around the delta cause expensive damage.

arcuate delta

Coast

Fertile alluvial soils – farming

The Nile delta

EGYPTIAN LOCATION

Mediterranean Sea

Nile Delta · Cairo

EGYPT

River Nile

Aswan Dam

Revision Summary

1) Name the four kinds of horizontal transfer in the hydrosphere.

2) Define the term 'drainage basin'.

3) What is a watershed?

4) Name the following features:
   a) the place where a river starts.
   b) the place where a river enters the sea.
   c) the amount of water a river carries.

5) Draw a storm hydrograph and add these labels:
   base flow, rising limb, falling limb, rainfall, lag time.

6) Where is the highest rainfall in the UK?
   Where is there most demand for water?

7) List five advantages and five disadvantages of the Aswan Dam in Egypt.

8) Describe the positive and negative consequences of these water management
   methods: a) afforestation   b) dam building   c) urbanisation

9) Write a brief account to say why the Lynmouth flood was so bad.

10) Describe an example of a flood in an LEDC.
    Explain why floods in LEDCs often cause bigger problems.

11) Explain the following terms:
    a) culverts   b) branching channels   c) relief channels.

12) How can changing land use reduce flooding?

13) What does the term 'drought' mean?

14) What is desertification? How do people make desertification worse?

15) Describe five factors which make the river Nene prone to flooding.

16) Give three reasons for the disastrous floods in Mozambique in 2000.

17) What is meant by lateral erosion, headward erosion, and vertical erosion?

18) Name and describe the four ways a river transports its load.

19) Describe the four stages of deposition in rivers.

20) What are interlocking spurs? At which stage of a river are they found?

21) Draw diagrams to show the formation of: a) a waterfall   b) rapids.

22) Draw a cross-section of a river meander. Add these labels: river cliff,
    point bar, strong current, weaker current, deep channel, shallow channel.

23) What is a delta? Describe, with diagrams to help you, the three main types.

24) What is the river Usk like   a) at its source?   b) near its mouth?

25) How does a headland and bay coastline form?

26) Describe how a crack in a headland can turn into a stack.
    Use diagrams to help you.

27) Name an example of: a) a series of stacks   b) an arch

28) Are beaches formed by erosion or deposition?

29) What is: a) a spit?   b) a tombolo?   c) a barrier beach?

30) Name and describe the four ways in which waves transport material.

31) What problems are associated with hard engineering at coasts?

32) Describe three ways that people affect rivers.

33) Name five interest groups that have an opinion about coastal management.

34) Describe how the geology of the Dorset coast has affected its shape.

35) Draw a location map of the Holderness coast. Label at least four settlements.

36) How do people interact with the Nile delta?

MEDC Urban Environment

Urban areas in MEDCs can be great places to live, with easy access to services and entertainment. However, an increasing number of urban problems threaten to destroy the quality of life of people living in MEDC urban areas.

Quality of Life is Not the Same as Standard of Living

Quality of life is different from standard of living. Standard of living is about the material wealth of a person or community. So a high standard of living means owning a lot of things and living in luxury. Quality of life, on the other hand, is about how happy and satisfied people are with their lives and whether they have access to the things they need.

People in MEDCs tend to have a higher quality of life than people in LEDCs because they are better able to fulfil their needs. However, some people in MEDCs have a poor quality of life whilst others in LEDCs have a higher quality of life — a lot depends on people's attitudes and opinions. There is also no clear-cut way to measure quality of life — it can vary a lot between different people living in the same place.

Traffic Problems are Common in MEDC Cities

The increase in car ownership and commuting means many MEDC cities have major congestion problems, particularly at rush hours. Schemes like park-and-ride and flexi-time aim to reduce congestion at peak times. Time is money to industry, so it now tends to locate on the edge of cities near main roads to cut down time spent in traffic jams. Pollution caused by traffic fumes is a problem in many MEDC cities.

Traffic problems in MEDC cities

Manufacturing Decline has led to Inner City Problems

As traditional manufacturing near city centres has closed down, it has left empty, derelict buildings. Modern industries need more space and don't want to pay for expensive land in city centres. It's also hard to attract new businesses to run-down areas.

High unemployment levels due to the closure of industry can lead to social deprivation in inner cities.

A derelict warehouse in Lincoln

Poor quality housing and lack of social amenities have made this problem worse in some cities.

The government has tried to tackle some of these problems with Urban Renewal Schemes aimed at attracting industry to older areas, and encouraging investment in new housing, amenities and employment. Also, 'gentrification' of cities aims to improve areas by the 'smartening up' of old, existing housing.

EXAMPLES

Urban renewal schemes
London docklands development scheme
Salford Quays development, Manchester

Gentrification
Newcastle, Glasgow and Islington, London have had old inner city housing smartened up.

LEDC Urban Environment

Cities in LEDCs are often poorly planned and overcrowded.
As a result, quality of life is usually lower than it is in MEDC cities.

Cities in <u>LEDCs</u> have their own <u>Land Use Problems</u>

<u>LEDC</u> urban problems are connected to the layout shown in the
diagram below. City layout is <u>not the same</u> in all <u>LEDCs</u>, but the
Latin American model is a good guide.

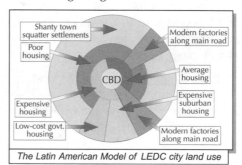

The Latin American Model of LEDC city land use

Notice that the <u>expensive housing</u> is found <u>near</u> the <u>CBD</u> (Central Business
District) — this is usually modern apartment blocks. The <u>poorer housing</u> is foun
<u>further away</u>, making the problem of access to amenities and work even worse.

<u>Spontaneous Settlements</u> are Common to LEDC Cities

Spontaneous settlements are a problem in many LEDC cities. They are also
known as <u>shanty towns</u> or <u>squatter settlements</u> (and many countries have their
own names for them, e.g. favelas in Brazil and bustees in India). These are
settlements built illegally by the very poor, who can't afford proper housing.
Most of the inhabitants are rural-urban migrants (people moving to the city from
the countryside). The settlements are badly built, without basic amenities.
Through time, the inhabitants may manage to improve their shanty town.

Shanty town accommodation in an LEDC

<u>Overcrowding</u> is a Major Problem in <u>LEDC</u> Cities

<u>Competition for land</u> is intense. High populations and lack of available
transport mean people want to live near places where they might find work.

Overcrowding puts <u>pressure on services</u> such as sanitation, health care and
housing provision. <u>LEDCs</u> can rarely afford to provide these services for all
— this leads to problems with clean water supply and waste disposal,
which can create <u>major health risks</u>.

The limited land available means that shanty towns are often <u>built on
dangerous ground</u> — for example steep hillsides which may collapse
in heavy rain, or on rubbish tips (a source of livelihood for some).
Overcrowding makes this problem worse.

Urban Socio-Economic Structures

Where people live in a city affects their quality of life. This page explains why different groups of people live in different parts of cities.

Economic Factors Affect Where People Live in Cities

The main thing that determines where people live within urban areas is personal wealth. People with a low income have to live in the less desirable parts of a city, where housing is cheaper. In MEDCs these tend to be inner-city areas, which are likely to be quite run-down, with poor service provision and urban problems like crime, traffic congestion, noise and air pollution.

People with higher incomes are more likely to live in better residential areas, usually towards the edges of cities in MEDCs. Commuting to work is very popular nowadays, so that people can live in the more peaceful, spacious areas outside the noisy and crowded city centre. However, there are also pockets of wealth in inner-cities, where areas have been gentrified (see page 41).

(see page 41)

> **REMINDER**
>
> **Gentrification** means the redevelopment of deprived areas, to make them into high quality luxury areas.

The Pattern is Slightly Different in LEDCs

In LEDC cities, the income-based pattern of where people live is the reverse of the MEDC pattern (see diagram on page 42). People with low-incomes usually live on the outskirts of cities — these people are mainly poor migrants who can't afford proper homes within the city centre. They often make up a large proportion of the city population.

(see diagram on page 42)

Higher income families tend to live in the inner-city, next to the CBD, because the highly paid office workers prefer to live close to where they work.

Social Factors also Affect Where People Live

Even though economic factors mainly determine where people live, people who share the same nationality, culture, ethnicity or religion often locate near each other in cities. This means that certain areas take on particular characteristics, depending on the main social group of their residents. For example, shops may sell particular things which are required by the local population, or there may be particular religious services.

> **EXAMPLES**
>
> **Areas of London where people of a certain nationality have located together:**
>
> | Urban area in London | Major nationality |
> |---|---|
> | Brick Lane | Bengali |
> | Stoke-Newington | Turkish |
> | Chinatown | Chinese |

Businesses are Spread Across the City Too

Where businesses and services are located also affects where people live.

The CBD is occupied by high-rise buildings and offices for businesses. Governmental and council buildings are also located in the CBD along with the headquarters of many companies. The price of land is high and there is usually little open space, so not many people live in the CBD.

Piccadilly Circus, part of London's CBD

People generally like to live in areas that have good service provision — for example people often try and live within the catchment area of a good school, which pushes house prices up in such areas. Also, some people might choose where they live based on a particular leisure or recreation service, e.g. athletes might want to live near to the stadium where they train. See page 46 for more on service provision in cities.

See page 46 for more on service provision in cities.

Urban Housing in MEDCs

Within urban areas access to different housing types varies. This creates distinct housing zones with distinctive groups of people living in them.

There are Different <u>Housing Zones</u> in <u>British Cities</u>

Although each city is different there are some patterns of housing distribution which apply to most MEDC cities:

- The <u>CBD</u> in the centre often has some <u>high-rise apartment blocks</u>.

- The <u>inner city</u> has many small, <u>terraced houses</u>. They were built during the industrial revolution in the nineteenth century to house factory workers.

- Some inner city areas have been <u>redeveloped</u> into <u>luxury flats</u> for city workers.

- There are often <u>high-rise blocks</u> on the edges of CBDs that were built in the 1960s as council housing.

- Medium-cost housing is found in the <u>suburbs</u>.

- The <u>commuter zone</u> on the edge of cities has the most expensive housing.

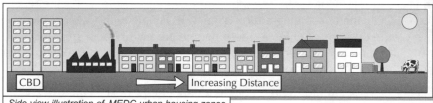

CBD → Increasing Distance

Side view illustration of MEDC urban housing zones

<u>Access</u> to Housing Varies

The main factor determining access to housing is <u>money</u>. Low-income families don't have much choice about where they live — they can only afford the cheapest housing. High-income families can pick and choose more. <u>Council house</u> schemes and <u>housing associations</u> can help house low-income families, but very often there is no choice about the type of housing or the location.

Access to Housing Affects <u>Quality of Life</u>

As money is the main constraining factor in housing access, people within similar <u>income-bands</u> are often concentrated in a particular type of housing.

- <u>Low-income</u> families are concentrated in <u>inner-city</u> areas — either the original terraces or the high-rise council flats next to the CBD. These are generally the most <u>deprived</u> areas, which suffer from social and environmental problems, like <u>racial tension</u> and poor quality housing. This negatively impacts on the quality of life of the people living there.

- <u>Middle-income</u> families are concentrated in medium-cost housing in the suburbs.

- <u>High-income</u> families are likely to be in high quality houses in the <u>commuter zone</u> or luxury flats in <u>gentrified</u> areas within the city centre. Expensive apartments in areas very close to the CBD have good access to many services but traffic congestion and noise affects people's quality of life.

Urban Services in MEDCs

There are lots of different types of services in one urban area. Services in MEDCs are usually linked to shopping, health, leisure and transport. Services in LEDCs are often more basic, such as access to water.

The *Distribution* of Services *Varies* Across Urban Areas

The main shopping area in an urban area is usually in the CBD. Corner shops and rows of neighbourhood shops are found within residential areas. Out-of-town shopping centres have developed on the urban-rural fringe.

Leisure services (like cinemas and gyms) are often located close to shopping areas. Many are located in the CBD, or in the newer out-of-town leisure and shopping complexes.

Public transport services are concentrated in CBD areas but tend to radiate out to serve whole urban areas. Good examples are the London Underground network which covers most of London and the Sheffield Interchange, where bus, train and tram services meet, a few minutes walk away from the city centre.

Open spaces are found in various different parts of urban areas, e.g. Hyde Park is located in central London, but Clapham Common is located in an outer suburban area of London. Small playgrounds and areas of open space are found on most estates and housing areas of the inner city.

Hyde Park, London

Educational services, like schools, colleges and libraries are found in all cities. Many cities are also home to a university, which usually has its facilities spread throughout the city.

Health services, like drop-in clinics, dentists and doctors' surgeries are found in most residential areas, as well as in the city centre, near shops. Hospitals are found in most cities, usually in places which are easily accessible for cars.

Some Services are *Easier* to Get to than Others

Access to services means how easy or difficult it is to reach them. How accessible the services are in an urban area varies for different groups of people. This affects their quality of life.

Access to services can be affected by a number of factors:

- People who live on the outskirts of urban areas have to travel to access the services in the CBD. This is a particular problem in LEDCs because the cheapest housing is often located a long way from the services in the centre and the poorest people find it hardest to travel across the city.

- The poorest people in cities struggle to pay for transport to access services that are beyond walking distance.

- Age and disability restrict access to services — for example, the very old and the disabled are unable to travel through cities easily, so they usually need help accessing services (e.g. an ambulance service often takes elderly people to doctor and hospital appointments).

- Out-of-town services like retail parks and supermarkets can be hard to reach unless people own a car. Access is restricted for people who have to use public transport.

Case Study

You need to learn one case study to show how access to housing and services can vary within one city.

Case Study: *Housing and Service Provision in London*

The map below shows how different kinds of housing and services are distributed across London.

Many people commute into London from towns like Watford, Croydon and Crawley.

New designer flats in Chelsea

Expensive and fashionable new flats have been built in Chelsea harbour.

Docklands redevelopment

Some inner city areas have been redeveloped into offices and attractiv[e] new housing for affluen[t] workers.

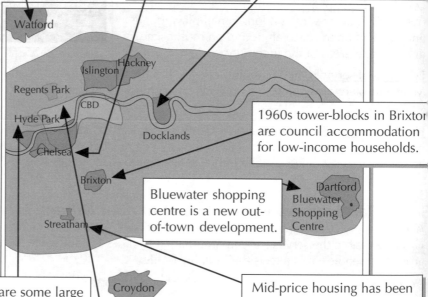

1960s tower-blocks in Brixton are council accommodation for low-income households.

Bluewater shopping centre is a new out-of-town development.

Mid-price housing has been built along the main communication routes in and out of the city in places like Streatham, which is next to the A23 (one of the major roads that enter London from the M25).

There are some large open spaces in the middle of the city.

The Main Shopping areas are found in the CBD along with governmental offices and financial centres.

Central shopping area

The Changing Urban Environment

There are many changes taking place in housing and service provision for a variety of reasons, in both MEDCs and LEDCs.

Out-of-Town Shopping Centres are Increasingly Popular

The Trafford Centre, Manchester

Out-of-town shopping centres and retail parks have become more common in the last 20 years. They are most attractive to <u>car-owners</u> because it is easiest to get to them by driving. The centres allow people to buy lots of different goods in a small space. Some people think that the new shopping centres are causing traditional town centres to <u>decline</u>.

TIP

The <u>Doughnut Effect</u> occurs when the commercial activity of a city becomes concentrated around the outskirts. Out-of-town shopping centres have become more common, so shops in the CBD have had problems competing. Some shops in city centres may even close down. This leaves a 'hollow' or empty area in the middle of the city. The effect began in the USA but is increasingly evident in British cities.

Trams have been Reintroduced in Some Cities

Trams were popular methods of urban transport in the first half of the nineteenth century. Recently, modern versions have been reintroduced in UK cities like <u>Manchester</u> and <u>Sheffield</u>. Trams are an attempt to reduce <u>congestion</u> and <u>pollution</u> in cities. They are more <u>environmentally friendly</u> than buses because they run on <u>electricity</u>.

A tram in Sheffield

Park-and-Ride is a New Way of Travelling into Towns

<u>Park-and-ride</u> has been introduced to reduce congestion in crowded city centres in places like <u>York</u>, <u>Nottingham</u>, <u>Chester</u> and <u>Oxford</u>. The scheme helps to reduce traffic in the centre. People drive to out-of-town car parks and then take a bus or a <u>tram</u> to the centre.

Redeveloped Housing can Change Communities

When old, poor quality housing is replaced by <u>modern developments</u>, residents are often moved to other locations to be re-housed. This can cause problems because people feel the <u>community</u> they live in has been destroyed.

Squatter Settlements in LEDCs can be Improved

Governments in LEDCs have recognised that people who live in shanty towns often have a very poor quality of life. A number of schemes have been introduced to try and improve things for squatters:

- Some <u>settlements</u> were <u>removed</u> leaving the residents <u>homeless</u>. This was unsuccessful because people had no option but to set up more shanty towns.

- Some governments introduced <u>self-help schemes</u>, where they provided building materials for the residents of squatter settlements on the understanding that the residents carry out the building work themselves.

- Some governments have built completely <u>new communities</u> away from the old squatter settlements. The new settlements have good links to the CBD, which means employment is easier to find.

EXAMPLE

São Paulo in Brazil and New Delhi in India are places whose squatter settlements have benefited from self-help schemes.

Rohini in New Delhi is a community which was built in the 1980s to house people from old squatter settlements.

Urban Planning

Urban planners in both LEDCs and MEDCs aim to sustainably manage the increase in demand for space and resources.

Planners try to Make Urban Areas <u>Sustainable</u>

In urban areas in MEDCs, planners often focus on giving everyone <u>equal access</u> to services and improving the housing provision. In many cities in LEDCs, the priority for urban planners is to improve access to <u>clean water</u> and reduce the number of people who are living in illegal <u>squatter settlements</u>.

Planners use the <u>Agenda 21</u> proposals, which follow recommendations from the <u>Earth Summit</u> in Rio de Janeiro in 1992 on making places locally sustainable. The following list shows some of the aims of sustainable urban development:

TIP

Sustainability crops up a lot in geography. Have a look at pages 81-82 for more examples of the issues surrounding sustainability.

- Encourage <u>economic growth</u> whilst protecting the environment.

- <u>Reduce poverty</u>.

- Improve <u>urban-rural links</u> and communications.

- Manage <u>resource consumption</u> (e.g. our use of electricity and gas).

- Provide all people, particularly the disadvantaged, with <u>equal opportunities</u> for a healthy, safe and productive life.

- Involve a range of <u>stakeholders</u> — local government, local communities, the private sector, national governments and international agencies.

Many <u>Interest Groups</u> are Involved in <u>Urban Planning</u>

The <u>Government</u> pays for <u>major</u> urban projects, such as inner-city redevelopments like the Liverpool Docks project. The money used comes from the <u>Single Regeneration Budget</u> and allowances from the <u>European Union</u> (<u>EU</u>). <u>Local councils</u> fund <u>smaller</u> projects like pavement improvements.

The regenerated docks in Liverpool

EXAMPLE

The Hammersmith and Fulham Regeneration Project is run by a partnership. Different members of the partnership come together to make decisions. They include people like local residents, members of the borough council and representatives from local businesses.

Different groups of people make <u>decisions</u> regarding urban change and access to housing and services. Most large redevelopment projects involve both the <u>private</u> and <u>public</u> sector as well as the <u>local community</u>. The most successful projects are ones where lots of <u>different groups</u> are <u>consulted</u> and people are prepared to make <u>compromises</u>.

Plans to Change Urban Areas Frequently Cause <u>Conflict</u>

Conflicts arise when people who have <u>different interests</u> share the <u>same space</u>. The <u>local residents</u> may have different <u>priorities</u> than businesses, e.g. local people in a suburban area might want increased transport facilities to the CBD whilst businesses might prefer to see increased links to motorways and other towns.

Often, the groups that <u>have access to funds</u> like businesses from the private sector, will have more <u>power</u> to influence decisions than groups with a <u>limited financial input</u>. For each project there will always be <u>winners</u> and <u>losers</u>. Good planning aims to give <u>benefits</u> to as many <u>stakeholders</u> as possible and provide opportunities for the area to <u>develop more in the future</u>.

Case Study

You need to know one case study of the planning issues involved in a new development. Newbury is a good example to use because it is a source of conflict between different interest groups.

Case Study: _Newbury Bypass, Berkshire_

The centre of Newbury was becoming very congested:

Newbury is a town in Berkshire in the south of England with a population of around 35 000. The town centre of Newbury suffered from congestion due to a large volume of traffic. The government gave permission for a bypass to be built to try and reduce the congestion.

It was also hoped that the improved communication link offered by the bypass would attract new development to the area.

The Highways Agency and the local council were involved in the planning of the new bypass (A34) at Newbury. There were public consultations about the bypass to try and incorporate the views of the local people.

LOCATION

The Newbury Bypass opened in November, 1998:

The bypass is nine miles long and runs to the west of the town. The bypass encouraged development, and unemployment in Newbury dropped because there were new job opportunities.

Building the Newbury Bypass was controversial:

A number of different stakeholder groups had opinions about building the bypass:

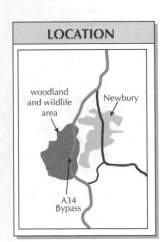
LOCATION

- Groups like Friends of the Earth and Greenpeace tried to prevent the bypass from being built. They thought it would cause too much environmental damage because trees would be cut down to make room for the road. Some sensitive wildlife sites were likely to be destroyed by the bypass.

- People who were opposed to the bypass tried to stop it being built by protesting. Some people protested by climbing the trees to prevent them from being cut down. Others used less direct protest like writing letters and signing petitions.

Removing vegetation to build a new road

- The local people who fought to stop the bypass development were worried about the loss of trees and the cost of £125 million.

- The police had to try and be neutral. They had to allow people the right to protest as well as protecting private land and property.

Newbury marked a change in new road policy:

Since the mid 1990s there has been a reversal of road building policy in Britain. Many plans to build new roads have been scrapped. Instead the government is trying to reduce traffic problems by improving public transport (e.g. introducing tram systems) and making the cost of driving more expensive (e.g. by introducing road tolls and increasing the price of road tax).

Population Growth

Population growth is a worrying matter. In some countries, the population is fairly stable, but in others, it's growing so <u>fast</u> that there's a strain on resources.

Population Growth is Affected by *Three* Factors

<u>Birth rate</u> — number of live babies born per thousand of the population per year

<u>Death rate</u> — number of deaths per thousand of the population per year.

<u>Migration</u> — number of people moving in or out.
(<u>Immigration</u> is people moving into an area, <u>emigration</u> is people moving away.)

The World's Population is <u>Growing</u> Very Rapidly

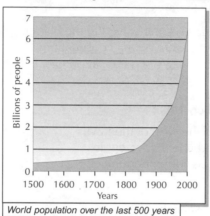

World population over the last 500 years

The graph shows <u>World Population Growth</u>. It's not just the increase that's important — the <u>rate of increase</u> is getting faster.

The 20th century has seen a <u>population explosion</u>. This means that a dramatic <u>drop</u> in the <u>death rate</u> has led to very rapid population growth.

The difference between the birth and death rates is the <u>natural increase</u> or <u>natural decrease</u>. (It's '<u>increase</u>' if the birth rate is higher and '<u>decrease</u>' if the death rate is higher.)

There is a Relationship Between Rural and Urban Areas

<u>Urban populations</u> are growing fastest in <u>LEDCs</u>. Factors that attract people to the city are job opportunities, improved services, better quality housing and a higher standard of living.

<u>Rural populations</u> are growing fastest in <u>MEDCs</u>. Factors that attract people to rural areas are clean air, reduction in traffic and pollution, more open space and cheaper housing.

A Country's <u>Economy</u> Influences its Population Size

In <u>LEDCs</u>, where a lot of <u>manual labour</u> is needed for industry, people tend to have a <u>lot of children</u> so they can go to work.
In MEDCs, where technical advances have reduced the need for labour, people tend to have <u>fewer</u> children.

Population Structure

Population structure is the number of males and females in different age groups.
It's often shown as a <u>pyramid</u> with males and females on each side and the
different ages making up the different sized <u>layers</u>.

Population *Pyramids* Show Population Structure

There are two basic population pyramid shapes.

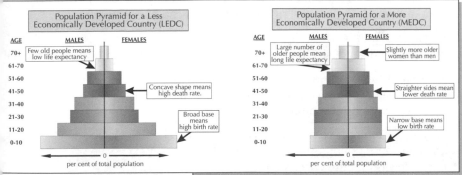

The two basic types of population pyramid

There are <u>3 common variations</u> on these basic shapes.

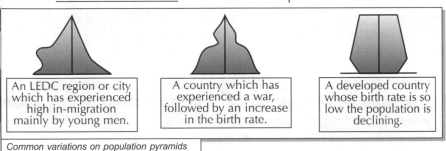

Common variations on population pyramids

Demographic Terms are Used to Describe Populations

A high <u>birth rate</u> or <u>death rate</u>, or a steeply rising population indicates an <u>LEDC</u>.
More children are born in LEDCs because less <u>birth control</u> is used.
This is due to cultural and religious pressure or a lack of contraception.

<u>Infant Mortality rate</u> — number of babies per thousand dying before
they are one year old. A high infant mortality rate indicates an <u>LEDC</u>.
This is because health care is worse in LEDCs.

<u>Life Expectancy</u> — the average number of years a person can expect to live.
A high life expectancy indicates a good health care system and an <u>MEDC</u>.

<u>Economically active</u> — people between 16 and 64 years old
(capable of earning a living). A high proportion of economically
active people indicates high earning power — an MEDC.

<u>Dependants</u> — people of non-working age supported by the
economically active. A high number of young dependants indicates
a high birth rate and an LEDC. A high number of elderly
dependants indicates a long life expectancy and an MEDC.

SUMMARY

**The structure of a
population is determined
by the proportion of males
and females and the
proportion of people in
different age groups.**

SUMMARY

Usual demographic features

	LEDCs	MEDCs
Birth rate	High	Low
Death rate	High	Low
Infant mortality rate	High	Low
Life Expectancy	Low	High
Proportion who are economically active	Low	High
Number of dependants	Many young	Many old

Managing Population Growth

Population growth needs to be <u>controlled</u>, because the bigger the population, the greater the demand on <u>resources</u>.

Increasing the <u>Food Supply</u> Seems Like the Obvious Solution

One of the simplest ways of meeting the requirements of a growing population is to use technology to increase food production. However, a lot of the techniques used to increase yields can cause problems.

<u>Irrigation of arid land</u> can increase the farming area. Schemes can be high-tech and expensive or simple and inexpensive, but can leave the soil salt

<u>Marshland can be drained</u> to increase the farming land. This is usually expensive and is mostly done in MEDCs, but these areas can be prone to flooding.

<u>Fertilisers</u> can improve poor quality soil, but can be expensive and can cause <u>pollution</u> — for example by allowing excessive nitrate levels into the water supply.

<u>Pesticides</u> can increase crop yield. But they can be expensive, and can kill insects and animals — affecting the whole <u>food chain</u>.

<u>Pressure on the environment</u> comes as more people try to produce food from the same area of land. The results can be soil erosion, desertification (see page 28) and deforestation (see page 13).

EXAMPLES

Problems caused by increasing food supply:

Colorado Scheme (Irrigation — USA)	Expensive; left soil salty
Tank irrigation (India)	Soil left salty
Polder Scheme (Draining of marshland — Netherlands)	Area has become prone to flooding

Sustainable Development can Slow Population Increase

To avoid causing long-term damage to the planet, the population increase has to be slowed.

LEDCs want to <u>reduce</u> the birth rate to slow population growth. To do this they need to break the <u>vicious circle</u> that causes the high birth rate.

The birth rate is influenced by <u>cultural</u> and <u>religious customs</u> which are very difficult to change. Many governments in LEDCs have encouraged <u>family planning</u> by educating women, opening clinics, and providing contraception.

<u>Population policies</u> aim to increase the standard of living by reducing levels of malnutrition. This is linked with health policies.

Vicious circle of high birth rates

EXAMPLES

Religious and cultural influences on population growth:

- Pope John Paul II has continued the Roman Catholic Church's stance against contraception.
- Islamic leaders are often opposed to birth control, and sometimes encourage the tradition of large families.
- Chinese culture sometimes values boy babies more highly than girl babies.

<u>Governments</u> Play a Role in Controlling Population

Governments can either <u>encourage</u> or <u>refuse</u> immigration into their country.

On a local scale, <u>planning</u> and <u>employment</u> policies will affect decisions to move. For example, <u>government grants</u> are often given to companies to locate in <u>deprived areas</u>. This encourages people to move to the area for <u>jobs</u>, increasing the economically active population, and <u>improving</u> the area's economy and status.

Migration

Migration is the movement of people from one place to another.

There are <u>Three Types</u> of Migration

International Migration — when people move from one <u>country</u> to another. This can be across the world, or just a few miles over a border. International migration from LEDCs to MEDCs is usually <u>economic migrants</u> searching for a higher standard of living.

Regional Migration — moving to another <u>region</u> in the same country.

Local Migration — when people move a <u>short distance</u> within the same region.

Migration can be Classified by <u>Reason</u>

Migration happens because of <u>push and pull factors</u>. Learn the two boxes below to make sure you know the difference. Remember — it's usually a <u>combination</u> of the two that causes migration.

<u>Push factors</u>	<u>Pull factors</u>
These are the things about the <u>origin</u> that make someone decide to move. They are usually <u>negative</u> things such as lack of job or education opportunities.	These are things about the <u>destination</u> that attract people. They are usually <u>positive</u> things such as job opportunities or the perception of a better standard of living.

EXAMPLES

Examples of migration include:
- **Economic migrants moving from Mexico to the wealthier USA.**
- **Researchers moving from the UK to the USA for better pay. This is known as 'Brain Drain' — highly qualified people moving away for better opportunities.**
- **Kosovan refugees moving from Albania to the UK because of war in 1999.**

Be <u>Clear</u> about the <u>Right Terms</u>

The words used to describe migration all sound pretty similar, so make sure you learn the difference between them really well.

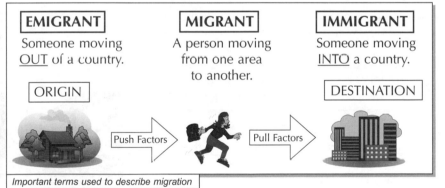

EMIGRANT	MIGRANT	IMMIGRANT
Someone moving <u>OUT</u> of a country.	A person moving from one area to another.	Someone moving <u>INTO</u> a country.

ORIGIN → Push Factors → Pull Factors → DESTINATION

Important terms used to describe migration

Governments Play an Important Role in Migration

Governments can either <u>encourage</u> or <u>refuse</u> immigration into their country through their policies. On a local scale, <u>planning and employment</u> policies will affect decisions to move.

EXAMPLE

Countries' policies for accepting immigrants vary considerably. For example, Britain's immigration policies are fairly relaxed compared with other European countries, like Germany.

Rural-Urban Migration can Lead to Problems

- Cities can become <u>over-crowded</u>.

- There is <u>pressure</u> on <u>services</u> in urban areas.

- Rural communities can <u>decline</u> because young people move out.

- Often people find that the <u>reality</u> of city life doesn't meet their <u>expectations</u>. In LEDCs many immigrants end up living in squatter settlements. In MEDCs some people find that they cannot earn enough money to live in expensive cities like London.

Counter-Urbanisation

Counter-urbanisation is the movement <u>out of cities</u> to the surrounding more rural areas. It has recently been happening in many MEDCs.

There are <u>Six Reasons</u> for <u>Counter-Urbanisation</u>

- <u>Growth in transport</u> and <u>communications</u> mean people no longer have to live where they work. Motorways and increased car ownership have led to <u>commuting</u>. <u>Government policies</u> can encourage movement out of cities, e.g. setting up <u>fast transport links</u> to 'satellite' towns and villages.

- The growth of <u>information technology</u> — faxes, e-mail and video conferencing — means more people can work from home.

- <u>New business parks</u> on out-of-town greenfield sites mean people no longer have to travel to city centres to work and prefer to live on the outskirts of cities to be nearer their work.

- <u>Pollution</u> and <u>traffic congestion</u> in cities encourage people to live in rural areas.

- More people <u>move to the country</u> when they <u>retire</u>.

- <u>House prices</u> in cities are high — people are moving out to find cheaper housing.

Counter-Urbanisation has a <u>Dramatic Effect</u> on <u>Villages</u>

Village <u>character</u> and <u>function</u> have changed due to the influx of people who work in urban areas. Learn this flow diagram, which shows you how.

> <u>Movement into village</u> of people working in urban areas who want to live in the country.

> A more <u>affluent population</u> and higher <u>car ownership</u> mean people use services in the city, <u>not</u> local services.

> An increase in <u>house prices</u> means young people can't <u>afford</u> homes and move away.

> The village is largely <u>empty</u> during the <u>day</u> — called a <u>dormitory village</u>. This leads to a decline in the community spirit.

Quiet dormitory village

> Local shops and services <u>close down</u> as few people use them. Rural transport provision is also <u>reduced</u> as it is non-economic.

> Local people without transport have <u>access</u> to fewer <u>amenities</u> — the young and old become <u>isolated</u>.

<u>Counter-Urbanisation</u> Changes Town and City Centres

When people move away from town centres changes occur:

- There is a lack of demand for services like local buses within the city.
- A decrease in the amount of money spent in the towns.

Planning and the Rural-Urban Fringe

Planning prevents the countryside being eaten up by new buildings.
This is called <u>checking urban sprawl</u>, and usually happens at the
rural-urban fringe — where the city and the country meet.

Urban Sprawl leads to the Growth of <u>Conurbations</u>

A conurbation's urban sprawl

<u>Urban sprawl</u> occurs when the <u>outward growth</u> of
cities is left <u>unchecked</u>, and the city gradually takes
up more and more of the surrounding countryside.
A <u>conurbation</u> is formed when one city grows so
large that it <u>encompasses</u> surrounding towns,
forming one huge urban area.

<u>Greenbelts</u> and <u>New Towns</u> — Checking Urban Sprawl

<u>Greenbelts</u> are areas around cities designed to stop urban sprawl. They were
set up around most of the UK's large cities in the 1940s, and building is
restricted within them. However, some greenbelts have now been released
for <u>development</u> due to the need for new housing.

Limiting urban sprawl meant there was a shortage of housing space in the cities,
so <u>new towns</u> and <u>expanded towns</u> were built beyond the greenbelt to house
the overspill population. This policy has been used in many countries,
including LEDCs.

The <u>Rural-Urban Fringe</u> Needs Planning for <u>Leisure</u>

<u>Leisure amenities</u> for urban dwellers are found on the rural-urban fringe because
they are easily accessible here, and need more space than can be found in cities.

Amenities such as <u>golf courses</u>, <u>country parks</u> and <u>riding stables</u> have grown in
recent years as increased car ownership has meant more people have access to
the countryside. <u>Farmers</u> have found that they can make money by expanding
into leisure activities such as '<u>pick your own</u>' fruit centres or <u>rare breeds</u>
visitor centres which provide a family day out. These facilities have
changed the character of the rural-urban fringe.

Planning has to get Clever when there's <u>No Room Left</u>

<u>More people</u> means there's a need for <u>more houses</u>.

- <u>Osaka, Japan</u> — Osaka is a very packed (10 000
  people per km^2), growing city with tiny houses.
  When all the flat land was inhabited, houses were
  built over the sea — this is called <u>land reclamation</u>.
  The new island provided more <u>spacious</u> housing
  with modern facilities and good transport links,
  <u>easing pressure</u> on Osaka city.

Reclaimed land in Osaka

- <u>São Paulo, Brazil</u> — Many poor people who move to the city for work end
  up living in favelas (shanty towns). A new <u>self-help housing scheme</u> is
  providing low-cost improvements. <u>Local people</u> do the work, and the
  <u>government</u> provides materials, electricity
  and sewage pipes.

- <u>Liverpool, UK</u> — An increasing <u>demand</u> for
  housing and government incentives for using
  <u>brownfield</u> sites has led to the <u>dockside</u>
  <u>redevelopment</u>, which provides housing and
  shops in a previously run-down area.

Liverpool dockland redevelopment

Case Studies

You need to know case studies on population for your exam.
Two big issues are managing changing populations and migration.

Case Study 1: *Population Management — China*

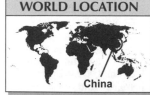
25% of the world's population is Chinese. In 1979 the government introduced a "One Child Policy" to control population growth sustainably.

The policy

Couples had to gain permission from family planning officials for each birth. Birth control was strictly enforced. People who had unauthorised children were given big fines. Authorised children were given benefits such as free education, health care, pensions and family benefits — unauthorised children were given no benefits, schooling or employment opportunities.

In 1982 couples with more than two children were forced to be sterilised (mainly women). Unauthorised pregnancies were often terminated by forced abortion.

Effects of the policy

The policy resulted in a high rate of infanticide (killing newborn children). 90% of fetuses aborted in China are female because Chinese tradition values boys above girls.

Recently the government has used less extreme methods (e.g. birth control education) with good results. It is estimated that without the policy there would be an extra 320 million people in China.

Case Study 2: *Rural to Urban Migration in Mexico*

Many people in Mexico move from the countryside to towns and cities such as Mexico City.

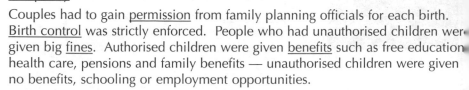
Push factors (away from the villages)	Pull factors (towards the towns and cities)
Lack of job opportunities. Agriculture is often the only choice.	Perception of higher standard of living.
Pressure on the land — land is sub-divided within families, leaving small plots.	Bigger range of employment opportunities.
Increase in mechanisation reduces the amount of farm labour needed.	Better education — larger number of schools and better facilities.
Lack of services, e.g. hospitals, schools.	Better housing.
Lack of investment in rural areas.	Attraction of 'bright lights'.

Effects of migration

Mexico City, and other large cities like it, suffer from severe overcrowding. There is added pressure on its services, especially hospitals and schools. However, the introduction of people from different places has created a social or ethnic mix which makes the city more 'vibrant'.

In the Mexican villages, there is often a loss of community spirit, as people move away from the area. Rural areas are often left with an elderly population as younger people move to the cities. However, there is less pressure on the land — which increases agricultural opportunities for those that remain in the area.

Revision Summary

Don't be put off by the size of this two-page revision summary. There's a lot to learn in this section so you need to do a lot of questions to make sure you've covered everything. Take a deep breath and work through the questions a few at a time. If there are any that you can't answer then go back and learn the facts some more. Keep doing this until you can answer all the questions — then you know you'll breeze the exam on this stuff.

1) Define the term 'quality of life'.

2) Why is quality of life difficult to measure?

3) How does quality of life differ from standard of living?

4) What is gentrification?

5) Where is the most expensive housing found in LEDC cities?

6) Give another name for spontaneous settlements.

7) Name two cities which have spontaneous settlements.

8) Describe some of the problems that are caused by overcrowding in LEDC cities.

9) How do economic factors affect where people live?

10) Why do higher-income families prefer to live near the CBD in LEDC cities?

11) Name two areas of London which have communities of people of the same nationality living together.

12) Where would you be likely to find high-rise accommodation in an MEDC city?

13) In what areas is medium-cost housing found in MEDC cities?

14) Why might low-income families have a poor quality of life in an urban area?

15) Describe the pattern of transport services in MEDC cities.

16) Name two open spaces in central London.

17) Where is Bluewater shopping centre?

18) Name four factors which affect the accessibility of urban services.

19) Write a mini-essay about housing and service provision in London.

20) How do park-and-ride schemes work?

21) What other scheme has been used to reduce congestion in Sheffield and Manchester?

22) How does the redevelopment of old housing cause problems?

23) Describe three ways that squatter settlements can be improved in LEDCs.

24) Give six ways that planners try to make urban development sustainable.

25) Where is Newbury?

26) Who was involved in making the plans for the Newbury bypass?

27) What are the positive consequences of building the bypass?

28) Who opposed the building of the bypass? Why?

29) What has happened to the road building policy in Britain since the mid 1990s?

Revision Summary

30) Define the following terms:
   a) birth rate   b) death rate   c) migration

31) Sketch a graph of the world's population over the last 500 years.

32) What is a 'population explosion'? What causes it?

33) Explain what 'natural increase' and 'natural decrease' mean.

34) Which are growing fastest in LEDCs — urban or rural populations?

35) What are population pyramids used to show?

36) Sketch a population pyramid for a country which has experienced a war followed by an increase in birth rate.

37) What do the following demographic terms mean?
   a) infant mortality rate   b) dependants

38) Do the following terms describe an LEDC or an MEDC?
   a) high life expectancy
   b) high number of elderly dependants
   c) high number of young dependants
   d) high infant mortality rate

39) Write a mini essay to describe the problems that increasing food production can cause.

40) Draw the vicious circle which causes high birth rates in LEDCs.

41) How can governments influence population sizes?

42) What are the three types of migration?

43) List some push and full factors which cause people to migrate.

44) What word is used to describe somebody moving into a place?

45) What problems can rural-urban migration cause?

46) What is counter-urbanisation?

47) List the six reasons for counter-urbanisation.

48) What is a dormitory village?

49) What effect does counter-urbanisation have on town and city centres?

50) What is a conurbation?

51) Explain why greenbelts and new towns were necessary.

52) Name a new town in the UK.

53) How has the character of the rural-urban fringe changed in recent years?

54) Describe the planning initiatives in Osaka, São Paulo and Liverpool.

55) What percentage of the world's population is Chinese?

56) Explain what the Chinese One Child policy involves.

57) What effects have the policy had on China's population?

58) List five push and five pull factors which encourage rural-urban migration in Mexico.

59) What effect has the migration had on the Mexican villages?

EXAM TIP

Questions where you have to comment on a population graph or pyramid can come up in the exam, so make sure you know what kind of things they are used to represent.

EXAM TIP

Using examples like Osaka, São Paulo and Liverpool will show the examiner that you understand how planning issues take effect in the real world.

Employment in LEDCs and MEDCs

The <u>characteristics</u> of employment in <u>LEDCs</u> are different from those in <u>MEDCs</u>.

Employment in an _LEDC_ can be _Formal_ or _Informal_

<u>The formal sector</u> is regular waged employment, usually <u>manufacturing</u>. Wages are often low and hours can be long, but it provides a regular income.

<u>The informal sector</u> is usually work in <u>small scale</u> manufacturing or <u>service</u> industries — where people <u>create</u> their own employment to meet local <u>demand</u>.

<u>In many LEDCs</u>, more people <u>look</u> for work in the formal sector than there are jobs. So the informal sector plays a vital role in the economy of many countries, <u>employing</u> more people than the formal sector. There is <u>little</u> or <u>no security</u> in the informal sector, and many people are trapped by <u>lack of opportunity</u> to improve their position.

	EXAMPLES	
Formal sector	Breweries Clothes manufacturers	
Informal sector	Florists Builders Delivery companies	

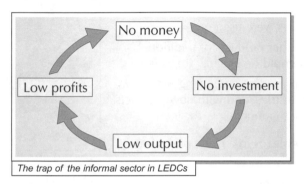

The trap of the informal sector in LEDCs

<u>LEDCs</u> have found it difficult to develop their formal sector, because they <u>don't have</u> the money to <u>invest</u> in it, and lack the <u>infrastructure</u> (power supplies and transport networks) necessary for success. Many large companies in LEDCs are <u>multinationals</u>.

KEY TERM

Multinationals are large companies that have branches in different countries. See page 77 for more on this.

Employment in an _MEDC_ is Typically _Formal_

In <u>MEDCs</u>, the majority of the employment is in the <u>formal</u> sector. From the wage people get in the formal sector, they have to pay <u>tax</u> and <u>National Insurance</u>, which help provide healthcare, schools and other public services. Most formal sector jobs in MEDCs provide <u>job security</u>, so employees can be confident that they will have a continuous wage. These jobs often allow employees to <u>improve</u> their position over time. Unlike LEDCs, where there is work in both the formal and informal sectors, in MEDCs there is very little work in the informal sector.

Unlike LEDCs, MEDCs have only a small amount of employment in <u>primary</u> industries such as farming. Most employment in MEDCs is in the <u>secondary</u> and <u>tertiary</u> industries. (See page 72 for more on the different types of industry.)

<u>Manufacturing</u> has traditionally been the dominant industry in MEDCs such as the UK. However, manufacturing is increasingly being relocated to <u>newly industrialised countries</u> (NICs) where companies are attracted by cheap labour, cheaper land and fewer tax regulations.

<u>Tertiary</u> industries now dominate in MEDCs. Health, education, transport and finance services are well developed in MEDCs. Such service industries have developed because they have had sufficient <u>investment</u>, <u>infrastructure</u> and <u>market</u>.

EXAMPLES

There are a number of NICs in South East Asia, including Singapore, Hong Kong, South Korea and Taiwan. Collectively, these are known as the 'tiger economies'. There's more about these on page 76.

Employment Opportunities

Employment opportunities can vary between different regions of the same country. They depend on a variety of factors, e.g. resources, location factors, communication links, market, cost and competition.

Some Areas have Suffered from Unemployment

<u>Northern</u> and <u>western</u> parts of Britain have suffered increased <u>unemployment</u> since World War II. This is due to the decline of <u>traditional industries</u> in these areas, which has led to a reduction in available jobs. Traditional industries include coal mining, steelmaking, ship building and textile manufacture. These industries were located in the north and west to be close to <u>coal supplies</u> as coal was the main fuel and was expensive to transport.

Traditional industries declined for a number of reasons:

- Coal reserves were <u>used up</u>.
- Coal and other products of traditional industries could be <u>cheaply imported</u>.
- The industries were <u>competing</u> with new, foreign industries, and with new products (e.g. plastics competing with steel).

Unemployment leads to a cycle of decline in the community:

Industries closing means that people are out of work and have <u>less money</u>. Less money is then spent on local goods and services, which leads to the decline of the <u>local economy</u> in general. When shops and services close, the area becomes <u>run down</u> and vandalised. There will also be a rise in crime and <u>social problems</u>. This makes it hard to attract <u>new industry</u> to the area.

Unemployment in the 1960s

Cycle of decline following closure of industry

EXAMPLES

Areas that have declined after a manufacturing industry stopped:

Location in decline	Industry that has ceased
towns in South Wales (e.g. Aberfan)	Coal mining
Sheffield	Steel-making

Other Areas have Experienced Employment Gain

In southern and eastern parts of Britain, there has been an <u>increase</u> in employment opportunities as a result of the growth in <u>industry</u> and <u>population</u>. The growth of <u>hi-tech</u> industries in business parks and industrial estates in the south-east of England has been a major factor in the increase in employment opportunities in the area. The south-east is a good location for industry because of its large <u>market</u> and good <u>communication</u> links with the rest of the country and with Europe.

EXAMPLES

Areas that have improved due to an increase in new industries:

Location	New industry
M4 corridor, west of London	hi-tech industries (e.g. computers)
around Cambridge	Scientific research (e.g. in drugs companies)

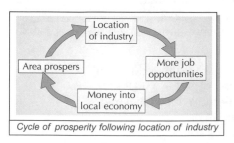

Cycle of prosperity following location of industry

An increase in job opportunities in an area leads to <u>population growth</u> and increased <u>prosperity</u> in the area. With more jobs, there is more money being earned and spent in the local economy, services are likely to increase in number and the <u>quality of life</u> for the locals is likely to be improved.

Changing Employment Opportunities

Employment opportunities are constantly changing over time in different regions and countries. They can be influenced by a number of different factors such as technology, investment and government spending.

Technology has Vastly Improved

The technological advances of the last 25 years have created both advantages and disadvantages for employment:

Advantages: The use of technology has allowed changes in industrial location. With improved communications and the use of technology, it isn't necessary to locate close to energy supplies, the market or other businesses. They can be part of a global industrial community without a specific location.

So, wherever industries now choose to locate, job opportunities in the area will be created, so industries can be persuaded to locate in areas of decline.

Disadvantages: The increased use of mechanisation and computers in industry has meant job losses and unemployment in the less skilled areas such as production line factory jobs.

Mechanised car production

Investment leads to More Employment Opportunities

Investing in technology has had a positive impact in many LEDCs. As a result of investment, there have been significant improvements in their secondary and tertiary industries and therefore an increase in job opportunities. Investment has also led to the development of some LEDCs into NICs (see page 76).

For example, India has established a National Information Technology Task Force. The Indian government encourages the development of technology companies by giving them tax relief. Indian exports of software are thriving and many service industries using IT now use India as a base (see page 62).

Government Spending can Improve Areas of Decline

Government spending is a factor that can affect employment opportunities. The government can choose to spend money on specific areas of a country that are suffering from unemployment or job losses. Both the UK government and the EU have regional policies to give financial assistance to areas with very high unemployment.

Nissan car plant in Washington

For example, the British government gave the Nissan car company a grant to locate in Washington in northeast England, an area of industrial decline. The new car factory provided new jobs. Local people who had suffered job losses from traditional industries had the opportunity to work again which brought money into the local economy. This had a positive effect on the community.

Case Studies

On this page are two examples of how employment structures have changed.

Case Study 1: Encouraging IT Development in <u>India</u>

In 1998, the Indian government set up a 'National Information Technology Task Force'. This was followed by India's individual states setting up their own <u>IT task forces</u>. IT companies are encouraged to develop in India through the government's special <u>tax offers</u>. No income tax is charged on exported services that use IT, and there's no duty charged on IT-related imports.

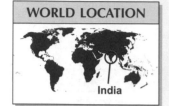

WORLD LOCATION

India

The task force has had a number of successes:

- '<u>Infotech parks</u>' have been set up to provide the advanced equipment necessary for the developing IT industry. For example, there is a hardware park near Mumbai, and software technology parks at Nagpur and Pune.

- <u>Education</u> in IT is improving. There is now an Institute of IT at the University of Mumbai, and there are a number of engineering colleges.

- <u>Communication</u> has been improved in rural areas through IT.

- Government offices are now <u>computerised</u>.

IT development has led to <u>increased employment</u>:

<u>Multinational companies</u> have been attracted to India by the government's incentives. India is now the base for many <u>service industries</u>, such as banks and airlines. Software <u>exports</u> have also risen rapidly.

These developments mean that there are now more <u>employment opportunities</u> for Indian people. More jobs are available in IT manufacturing, service industries and various multinationals.

Case Study 2: Mine Closure in <u>Consett</u>, 1980

<u>Consett</u> is a small town in the northeast of England that developed around a deep-mined coalfield. For employment, the area has traditionally relied on mining and heavy industries like steelmaking which used a lot of the local coal.

In 1980 the coal mine and the steelworks were closed due to competition from other areas and a <u>shift in energy supply</u>. The closures had serious <u>social and economic effects</u> on the local community.

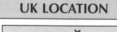

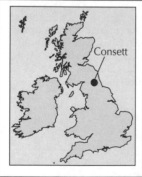

UK LOCATION

Consett

- <u>Unemployment</u> rose from 15% to 27%.

- There were effects on local businesses and the <u>local economy struggled</u>.

- Many people <u>moved away</u> to try and find employment.

- <u>Crime rates rose</u> and the town became run-down due to a lack of investment.

The <u>government</u> tried to improve the situation:
A <u>new industrial estate</u> was built on the site of an old colliery to try and attract <u>new industries</u>. The area has since seen a shift away from primary industry. A lot of the new businesses are in the <u>secondary sector</u> (e.g. Derwent Valley Foods).

The C2C cycle route

Some land around the collieries has new uses like <u>leisure</u> and <u>culture</u>. For example the <u>C2C</u> (coast to coast) <u>cycle route</u> passes through Consett. Sculptures representing the area's industrial past have been put up along the cycle route. Efforts to <u>improve the local economy</u> have had some success and <u>unemployment has fallen</u>. Despite these efforts the area has yet to recover fully from the closures of the coalmines and steel industry.

Measuring Development

Measuring a country's development is tricky, because there are so many indicators of development.

Development Indices — Comparing Development Levels

The following indicators can be used to measure development:

- Gross Domestic Product (GDP): Total value of goods and services produced in a year per total population. Gross National Product (GNP) is similar but includes invisible earnings like foreign investments. This is useful but says nothing about distribution of wealth — it can therefore be misleading. GNP or GDP per capita are therefore more useful — they reveal the total value of goods and services produced in a year per person.

- Life expectancy: Average age a person can expect to live to — this is higher for women.

- Infant mortality rate: Number of babies who die under 1 year old, per thousand live births.

- Calorie intake: Average number of calories eaten per day — at least 2500 are needed for an adult to stay healthy.

- Energy consumption: Weight of coal (or equivalent) used per person per year — an indication of levels of industry.

- Urban population: Percentage of the total population living in towns and cities.

- Literacy rates: Percentage of adults who can read well enough to get by.

- People per doctor: Number of potential patients for every doctor.

	UK	ETHIOPIA
①	GNP per capita $28,700	GNP per capita $100
②	women 77 yrs men 74 yrs	women 48 yrs men 46 yrs
③	6 per thousand	120 per thousand
④	3,317 per day	1,610 per day
⑤	54 tonnes	0.03 tonnes
⑥	80%	15%
⑦	99%	36%
⑧	300	32,500

Comparison of development indices for the UK and Ethiopia

Many of these indices are linked, and relationships can be identified — for example countries with high GDP tend to have high urban populations and consume a lot of energy. These relationships can also be used to identify a country's level of development.

There are Two Main Problems with the Indices

Some countries may appear to be developed according to some indices but not others — as a country develops, some aspects develop before others. No measurement should be used on its own — it should be balanced with other indices to avoid any inaccuracies.

Up to date information isn't always available — maybe because a country doesn't have the administration necessary to compile and publish it, or because they don't want the information to be available publicly. This can make comparisons between countries difficult.

Contrast in Development

Developed and developing countries have different characteristics around the world.

The World's Wealth is <u>Not</u> Shared Out <u>Equally</u>

The world can be divided into richer and poorer countries — <u>25%</u> of the world's population live in MEDCs and own <u>80%</u> of the world's wealth.

Wealthier countries are known as <u>More Economically Developed Countries</u>, or MEDCs.

MEDC city

Poorer countries are described as <u>Less Economically Developed Countries</u>, or LEDCs — they're also called <u>developing countries</u> or the <u>third world</u>. This term came from a time when MEDCs were known as the 'first world', the former communist countries were the 'second world', and the rest were the 'third world'.

The term <u>development</u> refers to how <u>mature</u> a country's <u>economy</u>, <u>infrastructure</u> and <u>social systems</u> are — the more developed a country's economic systems are the wealthier it is.

The '<u>development gap</u>' is the <u>contrast</u> between rich and poor countries. It's best shown by comparing the estimated <u>GNP per capita</u> of a rich and a poor country (per capita means per person).

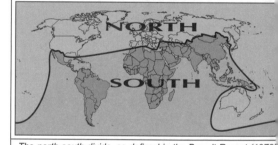
LEDC village

SUMMARY
Don't forget the exceptions in the north-south divide:
• Australia and New Zealand are in the southern hemisphere, but are MEDCs.
• Japan is an MEDC but has few natural resources.

The <u>North-South Divide</u> Separates LEDCs and MEDCs

The map of rich and poor countries can be split by a line called the <u>north-south divide</u>.

The <u>richer</u> countries are almost all in the <u>northern hemisphere</u>. <u>Poorer</u> countries are mostly in the <u>tropics</u> and the <u>southern hemisphere</u>.

The north-south divide, as defined in the Brandt Report (1979)

Places that suffer <u>natural disasters</u> like droughts are often <u>developing</u> countries.

The <u>richer</u> countries mainly have <u>temperate</u> (moderate) climates and <u>good natural resources</u>. This meant these countries developed their industry <u>first</u> and became <u>dominant</u> in the world economy.

The <u>explanations</u> for the north-south divide have as much to do with <u>political history</u> as they do with <u>physical geography</u>. Many MEDCs had <u>colonies</u> in LEDCs and there are still <u>restrictions</u> imposed on world trade — this means the development gap is getting <u>wider</u>.

This way of dividing countries into MEDCs and LEDCs can be praised for its <u>simplicity</u>. However, there are <u>criticisms</u>:

• The north-south divide defined in the Brandt report is probably <u>out of date</u>.

• It concentrates only on economic development and so <u>ignores</u> the complex <u>social</u> and <u>cultural</u> structures developed by many countries.

• Having only <u>two</u> groups (either MEDCs or LEDCs) is probably too <u>simplistic</u>.

Environmental Problems and Development

Many LEDCs have significant <u>environmental problems</u> that slow down the development process — lots of LEDCs are in tropical regions and often face hazards because of their climate.

Natural Hazards Cause LEDC Development Problems

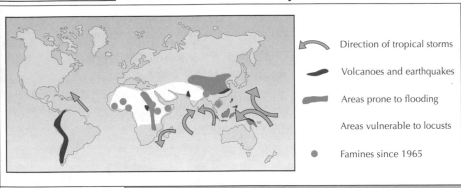

Direction of tropical storms

Volcanoes and earthquakes

Areas prone to flooding

Areas vulnerable to locusts

Famines since 1965

LEDCs and hazard zones

Large continental land masses have <u>extreme climates</u> and interior areas are very hot with long dry seasons. <u>Water supply</u> is a problem and <u>soil erosion</u> is a constant threat to farming.

<u>Tropical storms</u> like hurricanes, typhoons and cyclones <u>destroy</u> crops and buildings — repair costs can be enormous.

<u>Rainfall is uneven</u> during the year. Near the equator, communication links can be <u>washed away</u> in the rainy season — equatorial countries have wet and dry seasons <u>instead</u> of summer and winter.

Volcano erupting

<u>Natural hazards</u> like <u>earthquakes</u>, <u>volcanoes</u>, <u>tsunamis</u>, <u>droughts</u> and <u>floods</u> cause major damage in many LEDCs. <u>Poor warning</u> and <u>prediction systems</u> lead to many <u>deaths</u> and lots of <u>damage</u> to property. Farmland and development schemes can be destroyed or set back.

EXAMPLES

In Asia, monsoon winds bring heavy rain, which regularly causes flooding.

Tropical storms like hurricanes, typhoons and cyclones are common in Asia and the Caribbean.

EXAMPLES

Active volcanoes in LEDCs:

Country	Last eruption
Monserrat, West Indies	1997
Pinatubo, Phillipines	1991

LEDCs are Vulnerable to Two Other Factors

<u>Tropical diseases</u> like malaria spread quickly in LEDCs — the malarial <u>mosquito</u> is responsible for more human deaths than any other creature. <u>Water-borne diseases</u> like bilharzia are also common. Poor diet leads to <u>malnutrition</u> and diseases such as kwashiorkor (a condition affecting children) and rickets. <u>Bad sanitation</u> and <u>polluted water</u> can lead to typhoid and cholera. Recently, <u>AIDS</u> has been an increasing concern.

Mosquito

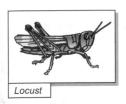

Locust

<u>Pests</u> are a problem for farming in LEDCs where farmers <u>can't afford</u> pesticides. One of the worst pests is the <u>locust</u> — a grasshopper-like creature that travels in swarms which can eat up entire crops within hours. Poorer harvests lead to a weaker economy, restricting development.

Dependency and the Colonial Past

The colonial history of LEDCs and MEDCs also helps explain the north-south divide.

The Colonial Period Established World Trade Patterns

In the eighteenth and nineteenth centuries, the developing world was colonised by European countries. The colonisers began by setting up trading posts but soon took control of whole territories.

Colonies provided agricultural produce not available in Europe, and were a cheap source of raw materials for European industry.

Colonies provided a market for European goods. The colonial powers made sure that their own colonies bought their goods — often at the expense of industry in the colony itself.

UK

Cotton is brought from India to mills in Lancashire — India is a cheap source of raw cotton. The British textile industry grows as a result. Cloth sold to India at a higher price than the cotton was bought for — profit made.

INDIA

Cotton bought at low prices and shipped to England. India forced to buy cloth from England at higher prices. Indian textile industry is destroyed.

The colonial trade pattern of the UK and India

A key result of the colonial era was the creation of a state of dependency — LEDCs rely heavily on MEDCs to buy their primary products and to supply manufactured goods. Most LEDCs are former colonies — they were never developed by their colonial rulers which means their economies are weaker and still dependent on the MEDCs who used to rule them.

Dependency Led to International Debt for LEDCs

The world recession and low interest rates on loans in the 1970s meant many LEDCs borrowed heavily from the World Bank and other sources to finance their industrial development. When interest rates rose in the 1980s, they couldn't repay these debts.

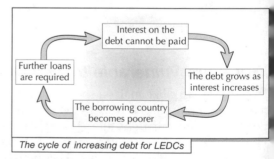

Interest on the debt cannot be paid

The debt grows as interest increases

The borrowing country becomes poorer

Further loans are required

The cycle of increasing debt for LEDCs

Rising debts mean many LEDCs have no money to invest in agriculture and industry, so development slows down. The only way out of the cycle is for lenders to cancel the debts.

Cancelling the debts would help MEDCs too, as more money in LEDCs would create a larger market for manufactured goods produced in the North. In the late 1990s, some MEDCs started cancelling some of the debts, but LEDCs still have a lot of debt to pay back.

International Trade

Trade is the exchange of goods and services between countries.
World trade patterns are an important aspect of development —
they seriously influence a country's economy.

World Trade Patterns Benefit MEDCs more than LEDCs

LEDCs have a relatively small share of world trade (except NICs),
and rely heavily on primary products for export income.

Primary products have four disadvantages for LEDCs:

LEDCs rely on primary products

- Raw materials have less value than manufactured goods.

- Prices are dictated by the MEDC buyers, not the producing countries.

- Prices fluctuate yearly and prediction is difficult.

- Man-made alternatives to some raw materials reduce demand.

MEDCs Rely on Manufactured Goods

Manufactured goods have a higher value and hold steady prices,
as the graph below shows.

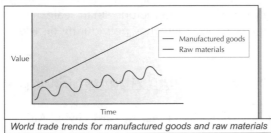

World trade trends for manufactured goods and raw materials

There are two important points:

- The price of manufactured goods is rising faster so the gap between the prices of manufactured goods and raw materials is widening — rich countries are getting richer and poor countries are getting relatively poorer.

- Prices of manufactured goods are steady, while prices of raw materials often fluctuate. This makes it difficult for LEDCs to predict their earnings.

Trade Blocs are Countries who are Trading Partners

Trade blocs are groups of countries with similar characteristics who have trade agreements benefiting the member countries.

An important feature of trade blocs is that member states don't charge tariffs on trade with each other, to encourage trade within the group — tariffs are taxes levied on imports to make them more expensive than domestically produced goods. They are higher for manufactured goods than for raw materials — affecting LEDCs in many ways:

- LEDCs can't compete — income from raw materials is low, and heavy tariffs are put on manufactured goods they produce for export to MEDCs.

- MEDCs can't lose — they import raw materials at low cost and put heavy tariffs on any manufactured goods from LEDCs, while trading freely between themselves.

So the current international trade system is not effective in narrowing the gap between LEDCs and MEDCs. In fact, it is making the problem worse.

The Question of Aid

Aid is the giving of resources (goods or services) — usually from MEDCs to LEDCs, either in an emergency or to promote long-term development.

Aid can be _Bilateral_, _Multilateral_ or _Non-Governmental_

Bilateral aid is aid given directly from one government to another. It could be money, training, personnel, technology, food or other supplies. It could be tied aid, which means the donor country puts conditions on the aid, usually to benefit itself. An MEDC can seem to be giving aid, but really be getting its money back and helping its own industry.

Tied aid

Multilateral aid is aid given through an agency such as the World Bank, usually money. The agency then distributes the aid to countries that need it.

Non-governmental aid is given through organisations like charities. This type of aid is very varied, and can include small scale development projects as well as emergency help during disasters.

There are Arguments _For and Against_ Giving Aid

In Favour of Giving Aid	Against Giving Aid
Emergency aid in times of disaster has saved lives and reduced people's misery.	Aid can increase the dependency of LEDCs on the donor country.
Development projects such as provision of clean water can lead to long-term improvements to living standards.	Inappropriate food aid can lead to a taste for imported food which the country can't afford and can't grow itself.
Assistance in developing natural resources and power supplies benefits the economy.	Profit from large projects can go to multinationals and donors, rather than the country that is supposed to be receiving the aid.
Aiding industrial development can create jobs and improve the infrastructure.	Aid doesn't always reach the people who need it and can be kept by corrupt officials.
Aid for agriculture can help to increase the food supply.	Aid can be spent on 'prestige projects' or in urban areas rather than in areas of real need.
Provision of medical training and equipment can improve health and standards of living.	Aid can be used as a weapon to exert political pressure on the receiving country.

The poorest countries don't always get most aid. Some MEDCs help LEDCs for political purposes rather than on the basis of need.

So aid can often create as many, or more, problems as it solves.

Development Projects

Development projects are schemes promoting development in LEDCs — often funded by aid money. They range from huge multi-million dollar schemes to small self-help projects.

Large Scale _Prestige Projects_ Don't Always _Succeed_

Some governments opt for prestige projects — expensive, well publicised schemes like dams providing water and electricity for large areas.

Prestige projects can be successful, but often they fail to achieve their aims. Some of the problems are outlined below.

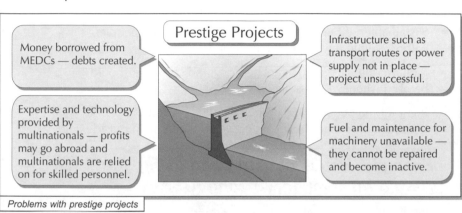

Money borrowed from MEDCs — debts created.

Prestige Projects

Infrastructure such as transport routes or power supply not in place — project unsuccessful.

Expertise and technology provided by multinationals — profits may go abroad and multinationals are relied on for skilled personnel.

Fuel and maintenance for machinery unavailable — they cannot be repaired and become inactive.

Problems with prestige projects

EXAMPLES
Prestige projects
Aswan Dam, Egypt
Gezira irrigation scheme, Sudan

Self-Help Schemes and _Small Scale Projects_ Lead to _Long-Term Development_

Small-scale projects are government or charity funded. They provide specific improvements for a small area and prioritise training for local people — which means they become self-sufficient, needing no outside help.

There are three main categories of small scale project:

- Provision of basic necessities to improve standards of living, such as clean water and sanitation, safe storage of agricultural produce or road building.

- Provision of essential services such as a health clinic or a school.

- Setting up co-operatives to facilitate low cost borrowing and saving schemes, run by local people to allow investment in agriculture or employment.

Small scale projects

Small Scale Projects Have Several _Advantages_

- Costs are lower and do not incur large debts.
- Training has long-term benefits for local people.
- Local people have ownership and don't have to rely on outsiders.
- Appropriate technology is used and maintenance is less of a problem. See page 70 for more on appropriate technology.

KEY TERM
Appropriate technology means setting up development schemes which are right for the people and the place. They have to be affordable and sustainable.

Appropriate Technology and Fair Trade

Appropriate technology and fair trade are both aspects of sustainable development that try to solve loads of problems at once. These new geography issues always pop up in the exams so learn them well.

Appropriate Technology Projects Follow Four Rules

To be appropriate, the technology has to be right for the people who use it and the place where it's used. Projects using inappropriate technology fail because they miss out one of the four rules:

- Affordable: The initial cost and any maintenance and parts must be cheap enough for the people involved.

- Sustainable: It must provide long-term use for the people, with very little impact on the environment.

- Right for the place: Local technology and expertise should be used whenever possible.

- Right for the people: The project should be what the people need. It also should be run by local people with very little outside help.

Example: House construction using straw bales — Navajo reservation, Arizona (USA)

Affordable: Straw bale houses provided the cheap accommodation that the local people needed.

Sustainable: They are long-term houses that have a low impact on the environment because the basic raw material is straw, not quarried stone. The bales provide good insulation so less energy is used in heating.

Right for the place: They have the baling technology locally and enough local labour to build their own homes.

Right for the people: The local people needed housing quickly — these houses can be put up in a day.

WORLD LOCATION

Arizona, USA

Fair Trade Gives Power to the 'Good' Producers

Fair trade is all about helping good producers survive against those who exploit their workers and the environment to keep the profits up and the prices low. It's an idea that could solve loads of problems at once — like bad employment practice, child labour and environmental damage.

- Products can be bought directly from the small producers so they don't have to sell to a large company who'll pay them very little.

Fair trade tea plantation

- Companies can appeal to ethical shoppers by displaying a fair trade logo. To put the logo on their products, they have to be good to the environment and treat their workers fairly — things like paying decent wages, banning child labour and improving safety standards.

- We often hear reports about children working long hours to produce things like footballs for well-known companies. This sort of thing will only stop if companies are forced to prove they're fair, by applying the fair trade rules.

EXAMPLES

Oxfam and The Bodyshop both buy products directly from small-scale producers in Brazil.

Fair trade coffee from Cafédirect displays a fair trade logo, showing their workers are treated fairly and they are good to the environment.

Case Studies

You need to know case studies about trade and aid.

Case Study 1: _Caribbean Bananas_

LEDCs rely on the export of primary products and therefore need to import manufactured goods. This interdependence of trade should ensure that all countries have the goods and services to meet their needs. In reality, there are problems because it doesn't strike a fair balance between LEDCs and MEDCs.

Some Caribbean islands (e.g. Jamaica, Barbados) depend on bananas for a large percentage of their export earnings. This is risky because if a natural disaster destroyed the banana plantations, there would be little to fall back on to make money from export.

In addition, the price of bananas can fluctuate depending on the stock market, so the Caribbean islands are never guaranteed a certain price.

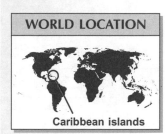

WORLD LOCATION

Caribbean islands

Goods sold in MEDCs have a higher price than their import price, so the cost of a banana in the UK is much higher than the cost of the imported banana. Out of the cost of a banana, only about 15% of the money goes to the Caribbean island, and only about 2% to the workers. The rest of the money goes on storage, shipping, advertising and profits to the company in the UK.

Caribbean banana growers

The EU gives favoured treatment, and a fair price, to the Caribbean for their bananas. Small farmers in the Caribbean need this because they can't compete with cheaper, mass-produced bananas grown on plantations in Central and South America ('dollar bananas'). However, the World Trade Organisation, which is in favour of free trade, believes that this favoured treatment is illegal.

Mini Case Studies: Different Types of _Aid_

Type of Aid	Example	Advantages	Disadvantages
Emergency Aid	Following an earthquake in Mexico, the Red Cross provided food, blankets, tents and medicine for the survivors.	This reached the people who needed help immediately during or after the disaster.	Only relief and short-term aid. It was withdrawn when the emergency situation ended.
Multilateral Aid	Ghana receives funds from the World Bank for small scale projects involving local people. This includes improving health care equipment, pest control, transport and tackling illiteracy.	Aid is organised by agencies operating under the World Bank. Funds are therefore distributed between projects fairly.	The large agencies organising aid are often slow to respond to the changing needs of people. Aid may also be held back if the donor country disagrees with a political or economic system.
Charitable Aid	Christian Aid, Oxfam, Save the Children and Cafod raised £15 million in 1994 to provide food aid for the people affected by drought in Ethiopia.	Money was provided both for emergencies and long-term development projects. There were no conditions on the aid, and no dependency.	If there is a disaster, aid is usually directed at providing relief for local people. This is only short-term aid.
Bilateral (tied) Aid	The UK funded building the Pergau Dam in Malaysia.	Money was provided for a large development project, providing employment, boosting economy.	Dependency was increased. Funds were for a large-scale project which was good for 'prestige' but did not benefit local people directly. Aid was only given to settle an arms deal which benefited the UK.
Long-Term Aid	The Catholic agency Cafod is helping agricultural development in Ethiopia. It helps provide wells, good quality seeds and drought-resistant trees. It is also helping locals to market surplus produce and set up businesses.	Future benefits for the local people, like lower chance of famine and local people are more able to support themselves. This funds sustainable projects.	May take some time before local people begin to feel the benefit.

Classification of Industry

There are <u>four types</u> of industry. They are classified according to the processes that take place.

Primary Industry *Involves Collecting* *Raw Materials*

<u>Raw materials</u> are anything <u>naturally present</u> in or on the earth <u>before processir</u>
They are collected in three ways:

- They can be <u>quarried</u>, <u>mined</u> or <u>drilled for</u> below the Earth's surface — e.g. coal mining and oil drilling.

- They can be <u>grown</u> — farming and forestry are both primary industries.

- They can be <u>collected</u> from the sea — fishing is also a primary industry.

Primary Industry

EXAMPLES

Types of industry

Primary	Farmer grows potatoes
Secondary	Factory processes potatoes into crisps
Tertiary	Shopkeeper sells crisps
Quaternary	Scientists research new production methods

Secondary Industry *is Manufacturing a* *Product*

A secondary industry is where a product from primary industry is turned into <u>another product</u>.

The <u>finished product</u> of one secondary industry may be <u>raw material</u> for another, e.g. one factory may make tyres which are then sent on to be used in a car plant.

Tertiary Industry *Provides a* *Service*

Tertiary Industry

Tertiary industry is the <u>largest</u> group of industries in <u>MEDCs</u>. It involves a wide range of services — anything from teaching, nursing and retailing to the police force or the civil service and transport.

EXAM TIP

Think of some examples of the different types of industry. Try to put them into a chain like the examples above. Remember, quaternary industry is less common than the others — it doesn't have to be part of the process unless the company needs new research.

Quaternary Industry *Involves* *Research* *and* *Developmer*

Quaternary industry is where scientists and researchers investigate and develop new products to sell.

Quaternary industry is the <u>newest</u> and smallest industrial sector, but it's growing rapidly due to developments in <u>information technology</u> and <u>communication</u>.

Quaternary Industry

Industry *is* *Not* *the Same as* *Employment*

<u>Industry</u> is part of a <u>chain</u> — from raw materials to finished product, finished product to service sector and service sector to research and development.

<u>Employment</u> is the <u>job</u> you do. So you could have a tertiary job as a secretary in a secondary industry like a toy factory.

Location of Industry

The growth of cities, population distribution and social and employment changes have all been affected by the location of industry. This page and the next page describe the <u>four</u> big influences on the location of industry — <u>raw materials</u>, <u>labour supply</u>, <u>transport</u> and <u>the market</u>.

Raw Materials Influence *Industrial Location*

During the Industrial Revolution, new industries needed <u>power supplies</u> (originally fast-flowing streams) and <u>raw materials</u> such as coal or iron ore. Industry grew up where these were easily available.

A pattern of industrial location developed where different areas specialised in industries using <u>local resources</u>. As most of our natural resources are in the <u>north of England</u>, this became our <u>industrial heartland</u>.

Location <u>near</u> raw materials reduces <u>transport costs</u>, particularly if they are bulky or lose weight during the manufacturing process.

<u>Ports</u> became important too, as they were the source of <u>imported</u> raw materials.

EXAMPLES	
Locations of industry	
Location	**Industry**
South Wales	Coal
Sheffield	Steel (particularly cutlery)
Newcastle	Ship building
Bristol and Liverpool	Ports

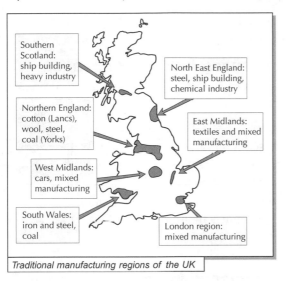

Traditional manufacturing regions of the UK

Southern Scotland: ship building, heavy industry

North East England: steel, ship building, chemical industry

Northern England: cotton (Lancs), wool, steel, coal (Yorks)

East Midlands: textiles and mixed manufacturing

West Midlands: cars, mixed manufacturing

South Wales: iron and steel, coal

London region: mixed manufacturing

Labour Supply has Influenced *Industrial Location*

<u>Availability of labour supply</u> is important to industry. A factory is likely to locate where there are enough people looking for work to fill their needs. Unemployment varies enormously by region, so this can be an important factor. The labour supply must be <u>suitable</u>.

There are three main types of labour requirement:

- <u>A large pool of unskilled labour</u> — some industries will <u>train</u> their own workforce in the necessary skills, and simply need a large group of <u>available people</u>.

- <u>A large specialised workforce</u> — some industries need a large workforce with particular <u>skills</u>, and they will often locate near <u>similar industries</u>, as the workforce will meet this requirement.

- <u>A small highly skilled workforce</u> — some industries need <u>highly skilled</u> or <u>qualified</u> staff, and will need to locate where these people are <u>available</u>.

Labour <u>costs</u> also vary around the country, so industries try to locate in an area where they can keep these costs down. Industries requiring highly skilled workers are <u>less likely</u> to be able to do this.

EXAMPLES	
Workforce requirements	
Unskilled labour	Processed food manufacturer
Specialised workforce	Car manufacturer
Highly skilled workforce	Scientific research laboratories

Location of Industry

This page covers more factors that affect the location of industry.

<table>
</table>

SUMMARY

Transport options

ROAD - convenient, flexible, specialist vehicles available, traffic jams a problem.

RAIL - cheaper, suitable for heavy cargo, restricted routes.

SEA - cheaper, slower, only suited for international transport. Good for specialist cargo, e.g. oil.

AIR - expensive, fast, suitable for small high value items.

EXAMPLE

For some UK industries who export to Europe, a location in southern England has become attractive, due to its proximity to their market.

KEY TERM

Industrial agglomeration: A concentration of linked industry in one area.

Transport Influences Location in Three Ways

The cost of transporting raw materials and finished product:
If the raw materials cost more to transport than the finished product (they may produce a lot of waste during manufacture, for instance) it is cheaper to locate near the raw materials. If the finished product is more expensive to transport (it may take up more space, or be expensive to insure) then the cheaper locatio will be nearer the market.

The type of transport used:
Traditionally, bulky cargo was transported by rail, so rail links were important. The increase in road transport in recent years has changed this. Many industrie are now located near main roads, particularly motorway intersections. Small high value items can be transported by air, but this is expensive. Goods destined for overseas markets are transported by ship, often using container lorries and roll-on roll-off ferries.

The speed required:
Some products need to be transported quickly, possibly because they go off quickly (e.g. milk). This may require a more expensive form of transport.

The Market Influences Industrial Location

The market is where a product is sold — usually a lot of separate places.

Location near the market is best when transporting the product is expensive.

When products are sent on from one industry to another it helps to be located close by. This leads to industrial agglomeration.

An agglomeration needs lots of labour in the region. A skilled labour force attracts more industries to the area. This means that labour pools and markets are often found in the same place.

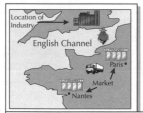
The influence of market on location

Other Factors Influence Industrial Location Too

Some industries are heavily reliant on large amounts of energy. These industries should be close to the energy source, or in a suitable location to receive imports.

Finance affects the location of industry — the cost of land varies from place to place. Also, more capital is needed for the larger industries.

Physical site affects the location of industry because some types of industry need particular sites, e.g. large factories need to be built on large, flat areas.

Another important factor is government policy. The government will encourage certain types of industry according to the social and economic conditions at the time.

The Government Affects Industrial Location in the UK

The British government is trying to improve industry in four ways:

- Setting up industrial areas (trading estates) and enterprise zones to encourage new industrial and commercial businesses.

- Encouraging companies to set up where there's high unemployment by giving incentives like cheap rent.

- Encouraging the development of derelict areas, e.g. docklands of London.

- Encouraging foreign investment into the UK.

Changing Industry — MEDCs

Industry in MEDCs has changed a lot in the last 50 years for a variety of reasons.

Traditional Manufacturing has Declined and the Service Sector has Grown

<u>Raw materials have started to run out</u>
Many natural resources have been used up and others are too expensive to continue extracting. Some materials are now imported from abroad.

<u>Competition from other countries has increased</u>
Many countries like LEDCs manufacture goods at cheaper costs than MEDCs can. This is often due to lower wages and poorer working conditions as well as less strict pollution controls.

This has Two Effects on Industrial Location

Many industries have <u>relocated near ports</u> where raw materials are imported.

New tertiary industries are often <u>footloose</u>, meaning they are <u>not</u> tied to a raw material location, and locate in pleasant environments near transport routes and near the markets (e.g. hi-tech industries like computing).

The Service Sector is now the Largest Employer

Increases in <u>tertiary industries</u> mean that <u>manufacturing</u> employs a smaller proportion of the working population. The pie charts show the change in the UK.

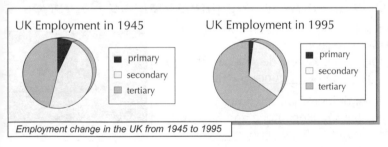

UK Employment in 1945   UK Employment in 1995

■ primary
□ secondary
■ tertiary

Employment change in the UK from 1945 to 1995

Footloose Industries often Locate in Science Parks

<u>Science parks</u> are estates of modern, usually footloose industries such as pharmaceuticals and computing which have grown up in recent years on the outskirts of towns. There are 3 main reasons for their growth:

The need to be near <u>raw materials</u> has been replaced by the need to be near <u>research centres</u> like universities and similar industries. Developments in hi-tech industry happen fast so companies need to be up-to-date to survive.

Land is often <u>cheaper</u> on the <u>town outskirts</u> than in the traditional central industrial areas, and access to transport routes is better.

<u>Information technology</u> is increasingly allowing hi-tech industry to locate further away from heavily populated areas.

Changing Industry — LEDCs

Manufacturing industry used to be mainly found in MEDCs, but this is changing

Manufacturing Industry has <u>Changed Location</u>

Over recent years there has been a shift in the location of <u>manufacturing industry</u> from <u>MEDCs to LEDCs</u>.

There are a variety of reasons for this shift:

- <u>Cheap labour</u> — A <u>hardworking</u> and <u>efficient</u> workforce is available at a <u>cheap</u> rate in LEDCs. This is one of the most important factors encouraging manufacturing industry to locate in LEDCs. Companies will be able to make a <u>bigger profit</u> if they are spending less on the wages of their workforce.

- <u>Lax regulations</u> — Companies often take advantage of <u>lax regulations</u> in LEDCs. <u>Health and safety</u> standards are often lower in LEDCs than in MEDCs, so companies can get away with spending less on safety. There may also be fewer regulations about <u>pollution</u>, so companies can save money through not having to use expensive pollution-reducing procedures.

- <u>Market</u> — Companies situated in LEDCs have access to <u>expanding markets</u>. This is particularly true in South East Asian countries, where many of the home markets have <u>developed</u> over recent years (see below).

- <u>Cheaper land</u> — The site for the development of the company is often <u>cheaper</u> in LEDCs than it would be in MEDCs, letting companies <u>save money</u> on land.

Some LEDCs are now <u>Newly Industrialised Countries</u>

Some countries, like the <u>Pacific Rim</u> countries in South East Asia, have seen dramatic levels of <u>industrialisation</u> in the last few decades, so they're called <u>Newly Industrialised Countries (NICs)</u>.

The greatest level of industrialisation has occurred in <u>South Korea</u>, <u>Taiwan</u>, <u>Hong Kong</u> and <u>Singapore</u> — collectively known as '<u>tiger economies</u>'.

The built-up skyline of Singapore

Although circumstances in each country are different, they <u>share</u> several characteristics which have helped this development:

- They <u>invested</u> in <u>infrastructure</u> during the 1960s.
- They have a <u>motivated</u> and <u>cheap</u> work force which attracted American and Japanese investors.
- They invested money very cleverly in new <u>hi-tech</u> products.
- They have a <u>large population</u> which is a <u>home market</u> for the goods.

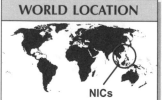
As a result, the <u>NICs</u> of the Pacific Rim have become formidable <u>competition</u> to the manufacturing industries of <u>MEDCs</u> and <u>no longer</u> have the characteristics associated with <u>LEDCs</u>.

There have been some <u>negative</u> consequences for the NICs. The manufacturing industry has caused a lot of <u>air pollution</u>. People's <u>health</u> can be damaged because of poor working conditions in factories. Also, relying on foreign investment means that economies are <u>unstable</u> when there are <u>recessions</u>.

Multinationals

Multinationals or MNCs (multi-national companies) differ from national companies in that they are large corporations with branches in several countries. They've grown huge in trade and manufacturing over the last thirty years.

Multinationals are Vital for World Manufacturing

Multinationals place different parts of their company in locations with the greatest benefits. Research and development (R & D) are usually located in MEDCs where research facilities and staff expertise are better. The manufacturing process is often completed in LEDCs or NICs where wages are lower, so production costs are cheaper.

Multinationals are extremely powerful. The largest — oil companies and car makers — have an annual turnover greater than the GNP of many LEDCs. It's estimated that in 1990 the hundred top multinationals controlled around 50% of all world manufacturing.

Many LEDCs try to attract multinationals by offering few restrictions on them, because they bring important capital investment into the country. This lack of restriction makes the multinationals even more powerful.

In the past, European and American companies controlled the global economy, but now the Asian companies are becoming dominant. In 1972 there was one Japanese firm in the UK — by 1991 there were 220.

The UK motorcycle industry was put out of business altogether at one stage, due to competition from Japan. Competition from NICs is also growing — companies like the Malaysian car firm Proton are increasing their share of the European car market.

EXAMPLE

The Coca-Cola multinational company

HQ	Atlanta, USA
Sold and made	In over 200 countries
Annual revenue	US$ 21 billion
Drunk by	A billion people every day.

There are Advantages and Disadvantages of MNCs

There are direct advantages and disadvantages of MNCs, and also 'multiplier effects' — knock-on effects such as education for workers' families.

Advantages

Multinationals.....
1) provide jobs and training for local people.
2) bring investment to the country.
3) provide expensive machinery and equipment which the host country cannot afford.
4) increase international trade and bring foreign currency.
5) provide health care and education for their workers and families.
6) increase wealth, providing a domestic market for consumer goods — which then creates more industry.

Disadvantages

Multinationals.....
1) provide mostly low paid jobs often with long hours.
2) bring in foreign nationals for management and higher paid positions.
3) take much of the profit out of the host country.
4) make products for export rather than for the domestic market.
5) can pull out of the host country at any time — the host may become dependent on their employment.
6) may pay little regard to the protection of the host country's environment.

The advantages and disadvantages of investment in countries by MNCs

Case Study

You need to know a case study of the location of an industry at a national scale and how its location has changed over time.

Case Study: <u>Coal Mining</u> in the <u>UK</u>

Most of the coal mining in the UK has been located in the northern and eastern areas of England and areas of South Wales. The <u>location</u> of coal mines has been <u>predetermined</u> by the location of the coal in the ground.

Over the last 50 years, there has been a dramatic <u>reduction</u> in the amount of coal mines operating in the UK. Many towns have seen the closure of mines and whole communities have suffered an increase in <u>unemployment</u> as a result. Cities and towns like Lancaster and Blackburn developed and thrived as coal mining towns but have since suffered <u>decline</u> and <u>deprivation</u>.

Aerial view of a coal mine

There are many <u>factors</u> that can help explain the decline in mining in the UK:

Reduction in the resource:

One simple reason for the closure of coal mines is that the coal is <u>running out</u>. Coal is a <u>finite</u> resource, and when the amount of coal found is so small that it no longer makes the mine profitable, there is little point in continuing to mine there.

Market trends:

Market trends often lead to economic change in an area (e.g. coal mine closure).
If the <u>demand</u> for a product falls, then it is likely to lead to a reduction in its <u>manufacture</u>.
In the case of coal, if demand falls, it leads to a <u>reduction</u> in coal mining. With more knowledge and concern about energy resources eventually

Wind power is preferable to coal

running out, <u>investment</u> in the UK has moved into <u>renewable</u> and more environmentally friendly resources such as <u>wind power</u>. Therefore, the demand for coal has fallen.

Competition from overseas:

Competition from overseas can also cause economic change in an area. This has been an important factor that has contributed to the decline of coal mining. For example, <u>importing</u> coal from abroad is <u>cheaper</u> than the extraction of the coal in South Wales. As a result, the demand for Welsh coal is reduced because it can be imported more cheaply.

EXAMPLES

UK towns which have suffered from coal mine closure include:
• **Swadlincote, Derbyshire**
• **Consett, County Durham**
• **Easington, County Durham**
• **Ashington, Northumberland**
• **Linlithgow, Scotland**
• **Aberfan, South Wales**

Ashington
Linlithgow
Easington
Consett
Swadlincote
Rhondda

EXAM TIP

There's more about the effects of coal mine closure on pages 60 & 62. There's also information on how areas which suffer from decline following coal mine closure can be improved.

Economic Activity and Environment

We humans interact with the environment in everything that we do. Sometimes human activity benefits the environment or is at least in balance with it. However, most human activity disrupts the natural environment in some way.

Soil Erosion Causes Long-Term Environmental Damage

Once soil is left bare, it is vulnerable to being blown or washed away. Human activity can cause soil erosion in the following ways:

- Deforestation removes roots and allows extensive wind and water damage.

- Ploughing compacts the ground and creates channels for rapid water flow.

- Monoculture and chemical fertilisers mean soil cannot recover naturally.

- Removing hedgerows and windbreaks makes soil vulnerable to wind erosion.

- Overgrazing leads to vegetation being removed faster than it can regrow.

Ploughing can lead to soil erosion

KEY TERM
Monoculture — **growing the same crop** **year after year.**

EXAMPLES
Soil erosion: **MEDC: wind erosion** **in Oklahoma, USA** **LEDC: erosion by** **water in Nepal**

Commercial Farming Leads to Habitat Destruction

Trees, hedges and meadowland are removed to make huge fields for maximum farming efficiency. This destroys the natural habitat of many wild creatures, and can lead to serious soil erosion. Overuse of fertilisers pollutes rivers and lakes.

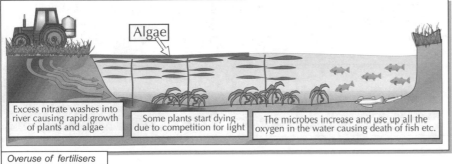

Algae

Excess nitrate washes into river causing rapid growth of plants and algae

Some plants start dying due to competition for light

The microbes increase and use up all the oxygen in the water causing death of fish etc.

Overuse of fertilisers

Pesticides disturb food chains and reduce insect, bird and mammal populations.

Tourism Causes Environmental Damage

The tourist industry has expanded rapidly in recent years, due to people having more free time and higher wages, and transport advances such as jet aircraft.

Mass tourism can bring environmental problems, e.g. footpath erosion and damage caused to sensitive areas such as tropical rainforest. Countries need to control numbers of tourists to prevent long-term environmental damage.

However, tourism brings increased wealth and employment — so many countries, particularly LEDCs like Thailand, encourage its growth without proper planning to reduce its effects on the environment.

FACT
Industry also causes water **pollution as well as air** **pollution, e.g. when waste** **materials from a factory are** **drained away into rivers.**

Environmental Conflict

There is often a conflict of interests between developers and conservationists. One example is the deforestation debate (see p.13), but there are others.

Tourist Development Causes Conflict in LEDCs

Game Parks are Wildlife Preservation Areas. The animals in game parks can be seen in their natural state — they are a huge attraction for visitors. Accommodation is often in tents and traditional buildings rather than conventional hotels. But problems can be caused if animals from game parks damage local farmers' land.

LEDCs promote tourism in game parks, but too many visitors can ruin the wild animals' natural habitat so they're forced to move to a new area.

Developments to accommodate tourists can also cause conflict because natural habitats are destroyed when facilities like hotels are built.

The demand for food by tourists can cause conflict because sometimes farmers are forced to expand their farms into conservation areas and destroy natural habitats.

Tourist Demands also Cause Conflict in MEDCs

Demand for access to tourist areas increases road construction and building of other facilities, often on farmland or open spaces.

Job-providing industries like quarrying can ruin a landscape that attracts tourists

Residents in tourist areas like National Parks might want new facilities like supermarkets and shopping centres which visitors and planners may think are not in keeping with the area.

Open land is often seen as recreation space, but it also provides farmers' livelihood

Some recreational activities are incompatible and can't happen together (e.g. fishing and jet-skiing can't happen together because the jet-skis would scare the fish away and the fishing lines could become entangled in the jet-skis

Conflict-causing events in MEDC tourist areas

The Use of National Parks Causes Conflict

National Parks are a particular source of environmental conflict in the UK. They are areas of outstanding natural beauty, and they are protected by law for the enjoyment of all members of the public. Much of the land is privately owned. There are many areas of conflict surrounding National Parks.

Planning regulations are very strict, and development is strictly controlled. Some industries in the area destroy the ethos of the parks — e.g. limestone quarrying in the Peak District provides jobs yet it destroys the very landscape that people come to see.

Visitors and tourists provide most jobs and income for residents, but cause traffic congestion, pollution, litter and footpath erosion. They can also cause damage to farmland and animals, destroying farmers' livelihoods.

Managing Conflict

Modern approaches to managing environmental conflict have focused on making economic activity sustainable.

Soil Erosion can be _Prevented_ and Possibly _Reversed_

Soil erosion is <u>avoidable</u> and may be <u>reversible</u> with good land management, such as the following methods:

- <u>Planting hedges</u> around fields to stop wind blowing the soil away.
- <u>Terracing</u> the slopes to reduce soil run-off and increase soil moisture storage.
- Using <u>fertiliser</u> made from cow manure, dead plants and food scraps.
- <u>Planting trees</u> that are good for building materials and for fruit.
- Using <u>branches</u> (not whole trees) for fuel.
- <u>Less intensive</u> use of land — letting it lie fallow to recover.
- Solving the major problems of <u>civil wars</u>, <u>below average rainfall</u> and <u>overpopulation</u> would help a huge amount, but these are harder to deal with.

Sustainable Farming Protects the Environment

<u>Organic farming</u> avoids using chemical fertilisers and pesticides. Instead farmers use things like manure as fertiliser and ladybirds as natural pest-killers. This causes far fewer problems for the surrounding environment. Yields are smaller so <u>prices</u> are <u>higher</u>, but popularity is growing, with consumers becoming more environmentally concerned.

<u>Sustainable farming projects</u> directly improve the surrounding ecosystems by impacting as little as possible themselves — this usually involves organic farming.

Ecotourism Reduces the Effect of Tourists

<u>Ecotourism</u> is a recent idea — specialist holidays for small groups living in <u>reserve zones</u>, eating <u>local food</u> and using simple <u>local accommodation</u>, allowing them to get really close to nature. Unlike mass tourism, ecotourism aims to be <u>sustainable</u> — causing as little <u>impact</u> as possible.

- <u>Small group numbers</u> means they can enter <u>sensitive areas</u> that others can't.
- These holidays are more <u>expensive</u>, so the income for the LEDC is better.
- Groups are <u>conservation-minded</u> and follow <u>strict guidelines</u>.
- Local culture and customs are <u>respected</u>.

National Park Authorities try to Resolve Conflict

These authorities have three jobs:

- to protect the <u>environment</u>.
- to promote the <u>enjoyment</u> and <u>understanding</u> of the parks.
- to look after the interests of the <u>residents</u>.

The authorities try to resolve conflicts through public <u>enquiries</u>.

<u>Planning</u> and <u>development restrictions</u> can control what goes on — e.g. 'park-and-ride' schemes can be used to reduce the numbers of vehicles in certain areas of a park.

Managing Resources

Humans need <u>energy</u>. We get it from <u>natural resources</u> converted into power supplies at <u>power stations</u> — usually in the form of <u>electricity</u> or <u>gas</u>.

Non-Renewable Resources May One Day *Run Out*

<u>Non-renewable resources</u> take so long to form that they can't be <u>replaced </u>once they run out. These include <u>fossil fuels</u> which have traditionally supplied most of our energy — <u>oil</u>, <u>coal</u> and <u>gas</u>. They are <u>not</u> sustainable and are a major source of <u>pollution</u>.

Oil extraction

<u>LEDCs</u> rely more heavily on <u>wood</u> as fuel. This is becoming a problem — population growth means increased demand on fuel, and leads to <u>deforestation</u> as more trees are cut down. This can also contribute to <u>soil erosion</u> as the earth loses tree cover protection.

Conservation and *Recycling* Provide for the *Future*

<u>Reducing demand</u> for fossil fuels means they'll <u>last longer</u>, and <u>reduce</u> the harmful <u>effects</u> of using them. <u>Conserving the soil</u> by preventing erosion will provide food for future generations. <u>Recycling</u> metals and paper means using <u>less raw material</u> and <u>cuts energy use</u> too.

Managing Resources is a *Balancing Act*

Some resources <u>aren't</u> always <u>available</u> where they're most wanted — e.g. the fastest-growing demand for water in the UK is in the south-east, but the highest rainfall is in the north and west.

There <u>won't</u> always be <u>enough</u> to go round — although <u>LEDCs</u> produce much of the world's resources, <u>most</u> are used by <u>MEDCs</u>. LEDC development means they want <u>more</u> resources.

Multinational companies fear that reduction in consumption will <u>reduce profits</u> — e.g. BP, which is involved in the search for new oil supplies off the Falkland Islands.

<u>Research</u> into alternative materials and energy resources is <u>time-consuming</u> and <u>expensive</u>.

Sustainable Use of Resources Needs Good *Stewardship*

<u>Stewardship</u> means using resources responsibly so some are left and so damage caused is minimal.

- <u>Resource conservation</u> — Using resources carefully to <u>slow</u> our consumption of them.

- <u>Resource substitution</u> — Changing resources for more <u>sustainable</u> ones.

- <u>Pollution control</u> — <u>Limiting</u> pollution to reduce problems like global warming and acid rain.

- <u>Recycling</u> — Used to reduce the amount of <u>waste</u> produced and as part of <u>resource conservation</u>.

You need to know a case study about the effect of an industry on the environment.

Case Study: *Heavy Industry in the Rhine-Ruhr region, Germany*

Location

The Rhine-Ruhr region is located in the west of Germany. It covers the <u>Ruhr coalfield</u> and is close to the river <u>Rhine</u>.

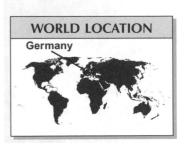

Background

The Rhine-Ruhr region of Germany developed as a prominent area of <u>heavy industry</u>. It was successful because of the high quality <u>coal</u> that was available and the large reserves of coal that could be used to provide <u>energy</u> for industries.

The coalmines provide <u>employment</u> opportunities for local people. But the industrial development has had damaging effects on the <u>environment</u>.

Conflicts

At the time of the coal mining, <u>visual</u> and <u>noise pollution</u> were a problem for local people. The mining created an eyesore and a dusty environment that would reduce the <u>quality of life</u> for the people living in the area.

As the traditional areas declined, the previously industrialised areas were left in a <u>derelict</u> state. The landscape has been left with <u>scars</u> from the removal of coal from the ground. This has proved to be a conflict as <u>conservationists</u> are concerned about the damage caused.

The visual impact of mining

Management

In recent years, the derelict areas have been <u>managed</u> and the idea of <u>sustainability</u> has been introduced into the area. The local authority has developed a programme of <u>improvement</u> to repair the damage caused by the industry. Most of the money for the improvements has been funded by the state, but there have also been contributions from private investors.

The main development involves:

- <u>Landscaping</u> the area that has been left with ground scars with the planting of trees and other vegetation.

- Development of the former industrial sites as <u>brownfield sites</u> to attract new industry to locate there and to improve the <u>employment</u> in the area.

- Building <u>new houses</u> on the land.

Revision Summary

There's a lot of stuff in this last section — employment, trade, aid, developmen
industry, the environment... It's all on the 'human' side of geography, so there
are lots of theories and questions and conflicts to learn about, rather than
straight-forward facts and diagrams. Have a go at the questions below to see
how much you've taken in. Then make sure you read over the bits you didn't g

1) Explain the difference between formal and informal employment.

2) Is employment in MEDCs typically formal or informal?

3) Which industry now dominates in MEDCs? Explain what it involves.

4) Which parts of the UK have suffered from increased unemployment? Wh

5) Draw the cycle of decline following the closure of industry in an area.

6) Draw the cycle of prosperity following the location of industry in an area.

7) Discuss how improved technology has affected employment opportunitie

8) How has investment affected employment in LEDCs? Give an example.

9) How can government spending improve areas of decline? Give an examp

10) Write a mini-essay to explain IT development in India, and its effects.

11) Describe the effects of mine closure in Consett in 1980.

12) How did the government improve the situation in Consett?

13) Name eight development indices.

14) Why is GDP per capita a more useful development indicator than GDP?

15) Explain the two main problems with the development indices.

16) What is the 'development gap'?

17) Draw a rough sketch of the world, adding on the north-south divide.

18) Explain three criticisms of the north-south divide.

19) Name two natural hazards and explain how they may affect development.

20) Draw a rough sketch of the world, marking on natural hazard zones.

21) Name two tropical diseases and explain how they are caused.

22) When was the colonial period and how did it shape world trade patterns?

23) Give an example of a trade pattern between the UK and a former colony.

24) How has dependency led to increasing debt for LEDCs?

25) List the four disadvantages of world trade patterns for LEDCs.

26) Draw a graph to show the value of manufactured goods and raw materials
over time. What does this graph mean for the development gap?

27) What are trade blocs? Give an example.

28) Describe three different types of aid.

29) Explain why tied aid benefits MEDCs more than LEDCs.

30) Write a mini-essay to discuss the advantages and disadvantages of aid.

31) Explain the problems with large-scale prestige projects.

32) How can self-help schemes lead to long-term development?

33) List the four rules of appropriate technology.

34) Explain why making houses from straw bales in the Navajo reservation was a project using appropriate technology.

35) What is 'Fair Trade' and why is it a good thing for LEDC producers?

36) Write a mini-essay on the trade in Caribbean bananas.

37) Give two examples of aid. For each one, describe its advantages and disadvantages.

38) Name the four types of industry, and give an example of each.

39) Explain how the location of raw materials affects the location of industry.

40) Name three regions of the UK and their traditional industry.

41) List three types of labour requirement. Which industries have which type?

42) List the three ways in which transport influences industrial location.

43) What is a market? How might it affect industrial location?

44) Describe the British government's incentives for industrial improvement.

45) Describe three reasons for the growth of science parks.

46) What benefits do LEDCs have that have attracted manufacturing industry?

47) What are NICs and where are many of them found?

48) List some of the characteristics of NICs which have led to their development.

49) What is an MNC? How do LEDCs encourage MNCs to locate in their country?

50) Write a mini-essay to discuss the advantages and disadvantages of MNCs for the countries where they operate.

51) Explain how market trends might have led to coal mine closure in the UK.

52) Name two other big reasons for UK coal mine closure.

53) Name five ways in which soil erosion is caused.

54) What might the overuse of fertilisers eventually lead to?

55) Why are some LEDCs not concerned about tourists ruining the environment?

56) Describe the conflicts that tourists cause in MEDCs and LEDCs.

57) What are National Parks? How do they cause conflict?

58) Describe sustainable farming and ecotourism.

59) What have National Park Authorities done to try and resolve conflict?

60) Who uses most of the world's resources? MEDCs or LEDCs?

61) Why are MNCs reluctant to reduce fuel consumption? Give an example.

62) Define 'stewardship'. List four examples of it.

63) Write a mini-essay on heavy industry in the Rhine-Ruhr region of Germany.

EXAM TIP

When it comes to questions about aid, the environment and unemployment, you'll often find a lot of useful information in the news. So make sure you pay attention to current affairs — the examiners will be pretty impressed if you can answer questions with up-to-date knowledge.

Ordnance Survey Maps

These two pages have everything you need to know about Ordnance Survey maps for the exam — <u>essential</u> if you want to get some easy marks.

Know your <u>Compass Points</u>

You've got to know the compass — for giving <u>directions</u>, saying which way a <u>river's flowing</u>, or knowing what they mean if they say 'look at the river in the <u>NW</u> of the map'. Read it <u>out loud</u> to yourself, going <u>clockwise</u>.

The four main compass points

Use a <u>Ruler</u> to Measure <u>Straight Distances</u>

To work out the <u>distance</u> between two features use a <u>ruler</u> to measure in cm and then <u>compare</u> it to the scale to work out the distance in km.

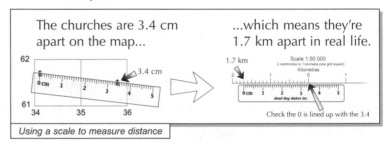

The churches are 3.4 cm apart on the map...

...which means they're 1.7 km apart in real life.

Using a scale to measure distance

Use <u>String</u> to Measure <u>Winding Distances</u>

To work out the distance between points along a bendy route (e.g. to find the length of a twisty road or river) lay a <u>piece of string</u> along the route, following all the <u>curves</u>. You can then <u>compare</u> the length of the string with the scale to work out the distance, just like using a ruler for straight distances.

<u>Grid References</u> Tell you Where Something Is

There are two kinds of grid reference: four figure grid references and six figure grid references.

Here's how to work out both, for the Post Office on this map.

Four-Figure Grid References:

Find the square you want.

Find the <u>Eastings</u> (across) value for the <u>left</u> side of the square (4

Find the <u>Northings</u> (up) value for the <u>bottom</u> of the square (70)

Write the numbers together. The grid reference is <u>4970</u>.

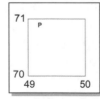

Six-Figure Grid References:

Start by working out the <u>basic</u> Eastings and Northings as abov

Then imagine the square's divided into <u>tenths</u>.
Divide it by <u>eye</u> — or even better use your <u>ruler</u>.

The Eastings value is now <u>492</u> (49 and 2 "tenths")
and the Northings is <u>709</u> (70 and 9 "tenths").

The six-figure reference is <u>492709</u>.

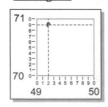

Ordnance Survey Maps

This page continues the stuff you need to know about using OS maps.

Relief is Shown by Contours and Spot Heights

Contours are those orange lines on Ordnance Survey maps.
They're imaginary lines joining points of equal height above sea-level.

If a map has lots of contour lines on it, it's a hilly or mountainous area.
If there are only a few contour lines, it'll be flat, and usually low-lying.

The steeper the slope is, the closer the contours get.
The flatter it is, the more spaced out they are. Look at these examples:

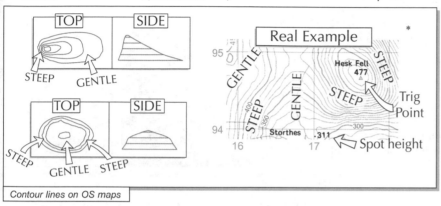

Contour lines on OS maps

A spot height is a dot giving the height of a particular place.
A trigonometrical point (trig point) is a blue triangle plus a height value, showing the highest point in an area (in metres).

Sketching Maps — do it Carefully

In the exam, they can give you a printed map and tell you to copy part of it onto an empty grid. Pretty straightforward, but you've got to get it right.

Make sure you read what bit they want you to draw out, and double check.
It might be only part of a lake or a wood, or only one of the roads.

EXAMPLE: *Q: Sketch the lake and the main roads and rivers on this map.*

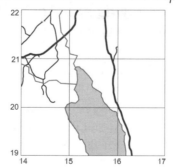

- Get the right shapes in the right place in the squares.

- It's a good idea to measure a few of the important points to help you — if you copy a few things over really accurately then filling in the other bits will be easier.

- Get the widths of the roads right.

- Draw your sketch in pencil so you can rub it out if it's wrong.

Drawing sketch maps

Human Geography — Plans and Photos

Plans, like maps, show places from above.
And like maps, there are a few <u>tricks</u> you need to learn.

Look at the Shapes when you Compare <u>Plans</u> and <u>Photo</u>

The simplest question they could ask you is something like *"Name the place labelled A on the photo"*.   Names are on the <u>plan</u>, so you've got to work out how the photo <u>matches</u> the plan.

Look for the main <u>features</u> on the <u>photo</u> and find them on the <u>plan</u> — things with an interesting <u>shape</u> like a <u>lake</u>, or big <u>roads</u> and <u>railways</u>.

EXAMPLE ONE:

> Photograph of St. James Harbour, 1986   Plan of St. James Harbour, 1984
>
> Q: Name the place labelled A on the photo.
>
> A: By the <u>shape</u> of the land, it's either got to be <u>Hope Point</u> or <u>Dead Dog Point</u>.
>
> There isn't a <u>road</u> or <u>building</u> at point A, so it <u>can't</u> be Dead Dog Point — it <u>must</u> be Hope Point.

Comparing photographs and plans

EXAM TIP

If you are asked to look at plans and photos in the exam be aware that they might not be the <u>same way up</u>. Spend a bit of time working out which way up they need to be so you don't get too confused.

The other type of question is when they ask <u>what's changed</u> between the photo and the plan, and <u>why</u>. Look at the shapes to find <u>what's</u> changed, then look at what it's being <u>used for now</u> (check the dates).

EXAMPLE TWO:

> Q: Where has land been reclaimed from the sea? Why has this been done?
>
> A: By the <u>shape</u> of the land, it's got to be <u>Baldy Bay</u> — the sea's further from that building now. It's being used as a car park, so they must have needed more parking.

A typical question about change over time

Plans of <u>Towns</u> and <u>Aerial Photos</u> — Look at the Buildings

When you get a <u>plan</u> in the exam, start by looking at the <u>types of buildings</u> and what's <u>around</u> them.

<u>Small</u> buildings are probably <u>houses</u> or <u>shops</u>.
<u>Bigger</u> buildings are probably <u>factories</u> or <u>schools</u>.

Work out what <u>kind of area</u> it is — lots of <u>car parks</u> and <u>shops</u> mean it's a <u>CBD</u>, <u>houses</u> with <u>gardens</u> mean a <u>residential area</u>, a <u>group of houses</u> surrounded by <u>fields</u> means a <u>village</u>. Always read the <u>labels</u>, they can give you a lot of easy c

EXAMPLE:

> This area has <u>houses</u> with front and back <u>gardens</u>, a <u>park</u>, a <u>school</u> and a <u>college</u>. So it's a <u>residential area</u> — you can tell it's <u>not</u> a CBD and <u>not</u> dense inner-city housing.

<u>AERIAL PHOTOS</u>: if you get an aerial photo instead of a plan, treat it in exactly the same way — look for <u>types of buildings</u> and what <u>kind of area</u> it is.
You can see the cars and trees which helps, but there won't be any <u>labels</u>.

Describing Maps and Charts

Describing <u>distributions</u> and <u>photos</u> can seem tricky,
but it's pretty easy once you've got the hang of it.

Distribution on Maps — Keep it Simple

This is an example of the type of question you might get:

> *Q:* *Use the map to describe the distribution of areas with*
> *a population density less than 10 persons per km².*
>
> Questions like this aren't easy — you can <u>see</u>
> where those pale yellow patches are, but putting
> it into <u>words</u> seems silly. <u>Don't panic</u> — just
> write down <u>a description of where things are</u>.
>
> *A:* The areas with a population density less than
> 10 persons per km² are distributed in the <u>north of Scotland</u>,
> the <u>north</u> and <u>south-west</u> of <u>England</u>, and <u>northern Wales</u>.

Less than 10 persons per km²
10 to 200 persons per km²
More than 200 persons per km²

A typical question about distribution on maps

Another worked example:

> *Q:* *Use the maps to describe the distribution of National Parks in Spondovia.*
>
> They've given you <u>two maps</u>, which
> means they want you to look at them
> <u>both</u>. Look at the <u>first map</u> and say <u>where</u>
> <u>the blobs are</u>, then look at the <u>second</u>
> <u>map</u> and say <u>if there's any link</u> or not:
>
> *A:* The National Parks are distributed in the <u>south-west</u> and <u>north-east</u>
> of Spondovia. They are all located in <u>mountainous</u> areas.

Spondovia

Key: ■ National Parks

Spondovia

Key: □ Mountains

A typical question describing distributions

Describing Photos — Check What They Want You To Do

<u>Double-check</u> what the question's asking. <u>Don't</u> tell them <u>everything</u>
if they <u>only</u> want what you <u>can see</u> from the photo — you <u>won't</u> get
the marks. Look at these two EXAMPLES for this photo:

> *The photo shows a 'honeypot'.*
> *List the factors that attract tourists to honeypot locations.*
> This is asking you to tell them <u>everything</u> you know.
>
> *The photo shows a 'honeypot'.*
> *List three factors that would attract tourists to this location.*
> This is asking you to list <u>only</u> the things you can
> <u>see</u> in <u>this photo</u>.

If they're asking you what you can <u>see</u> in the photo, then <u>don't over-complicate</u>
things — stick to what you can <u>see</u> in the photo. For example, if they asked
how <u>people</u> are affecting <u>erosion</u> of cliffs in this photo, then it's by <u>walking</u> on
them (the footpath), <u>not</u> the cars causing acid rain or something.

When you get a photo, look for <u>physical geography stuff</u> (what the land's like),
e.g. <u>coastal features</u> and <u>river features</u>, and the <u>human geography stuff</u>
(what the land is used for) e.g. the types of <u>buildings</u>, if there are any <u>car parks</u>,
if there are <u>roads</u> or <u>paths</u>, etc.

Use your head — for example if it <u>looks nice</u> and there's a <u>car park</u>,
you can guess there'll be <u>tourism</u>.

Typical questions about describing photographs

EXAM TIP

Describe places using
the compass points —
it's the easiest way to
make sure the examiner
knows which area you
are talking about.

North

West — East

South

EXAM TIP

Remember to double-
check whether they want
you to describe what you
can see in the photo or to
talk about something in a
wider sense.

KEY TERM

A <u>honeypot</u> is a
recreational area which
attracts a very large
number of visitors to a
relatively small space.

Types of Graphs and Charts

Two things you need to be able to do here. Number one: know how to <u>read</u> all of the types of graphs. Number two: know how to <u>fill in</u> all of the types of graphs. It's exactly what you have to do in the <u>exam</u>.

Bar Charts — Draw the Bars <u>Straight</u> and <u>Neat</u>

<u>How to Read Bar Charts</u>
Read along the <u>bottom</u> to find the <u>bar</u> you want.
Read from the <u>top</u> of the bar across to the <u>scale</u>, and read off the number.

EXAMPLE:
Q: *How many tonnes of oil does Russia produce per year?*

A: Go up the Russia bar, read across, and it's about 620 on the scale — but the scale's in thousands of tonnes, so the answer is <u>620 000 tonnes</u>.

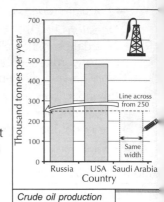

Crude oil production

<u>How to Fill in Bar Charts</u>

First find the number you want on the <u>vertical scale</u>.
With a <u>ruler</u>, trace a line across and draw in a bar of the <u>right size</u>.

EXAMPLE:
Q: *Complete the graph to show that Saudi Arabia produces 250 thousand tonnes of crude oil per year.*

A: Find 250 on the scale, trace a line across, then draw the bar in, the <u>same width</u> as the others.

Line Graphs — the Points are Joined by <u>Lines</u>

<u>How to Read Line Graphs</u>
Read along the <u>bottom</u> to find the number you want.
Read up to the line you want, then read across to the <u>vertical scale</u>.
EXAMPLE:

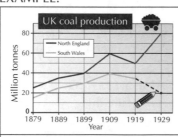

Q: *How much coal did the north of England produce in 1919?*

A: Find 1919, go up to the purple line, read across, and it's 50 on the scale. The scale's in millions of tonnes, so the answer is <u>50 million tonnes</u>.

An example question about UK coal production

<u>How to Fill in Line Graphs</u>
Find the value you want on the <u>bottom scale</u>.
Go up to get the right value on the <u>vertical scale</u>.
<u>Double-check</u> you're still at the right value from the <u>bottom</u>, then make a <u>mark</u>.
Using a <u>ruler</u>, join the mark to the line.

EXAMPLE:
Q: *Complete the graph to show that South Wales produced 20 million tonnes of coa in 1929.*

A: Find 1929 on the bottom, then go up to 20 million tonnes and make a mark then join it to the green line <u>with a ruler</u>.

Types of Graphs and Charts

Pie charts and triangular graphs are both ways of showing <u>percentages</u>.

Pie Charts Show Percentages

How to Read Pie Charts

Read numbers off a pie chart with a scale like this:

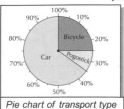

Pie chart of transport type

To work out the % for a wedge, write down where it <u>starts</u> and <u>ends</u>, then <u>subtract</u>.

For example, the 'Car' wedge goes from 35% to 100%: 100 − 35 = <u>65%</u>

They can ask you to <u>estimate</u> the percentage on a pie chart <u>without a scale</u>, but they'll only give you <u>easy</u> ones:

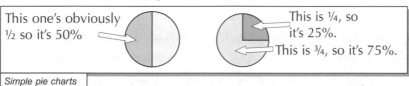

This one's obviously ½ so it's 50%

This is ¼, so it's 25%.

This is ¾, so it's 75%.

Simple pie charts

How to Fill In Pie Charts

With a <u>ruler</u>, draw lines from the <u>centre</u> to <u>0%</u>, and to the number on the <u>outside</u> that you want. Here's how you'd do <u>45%</u>:

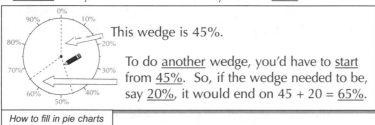

How to fill in pie charts

This wedge is 45%.

To do <u>another</u> wedge, you'd have to <u>start</u> from <u>45%</u>. So, if the wedge needed to be, say <u>20%</u>, it would end on 45 + 20 = <u>65%</u>.

Triangular Graphs Show Percentages too — on 3 Axes

Triangular graphs look terrible but they're actually fairly <u>easy</u> to use.

How to Read Triangular Graphs

Find the point you want on the graph.
<u>Turn the paper</u> so that one set of numbers is the <u>right way up</u>. Follow the lines <u>straight across</u> to that set of numbers, and write it down. Keep turning the paper round for <u>each set</u> of numbers.
<u>Double-check</u> that the numbers you've written down add up to 100%.

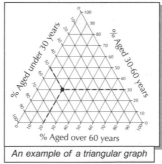

An example of a triangular graph

EXAMPLE:
The red point shows a population where <u>50%</u> are aged under 30, <u>30%</u> aged 30-60, and <u>20%</u> aged over 60. Double-check they add up to 100%: 50 + 30 + 20 = 100%.

How to Fill in Triangular Graphs

Start with <u>one set</u> of numbers — <u>turn the paper round</u> till they're the right way up.
Find the number you want, then draw a <u>faint pencil line</u> straight across.
Do the same for the other sets of numbers, <u>turning the paper round</u> each time.
Where your three lines <u>meet</u>, draw a <u>dot</u>.
<u>Double-check</u> your dot's in the right place.

FACT

Another type of graph is a <u>star graph</u>. Star graphs aren't as common as the other graphs on this page. They're really simple — just lots of axes arranged in a star shape. They're often used to display information like opinions and preferences, on a scale of 1 to 5 for example.

Attractiveness of villages, on a scale of 1 to 5

EXAM TIP

Triangle graphs don't crop up very often. If you get one in the exam the secret is to <u>turn the paper round</u> each time you read a different axis.

FACT

One of the most common uses of triangle graphs is to show the percentages of sand, silt and clay in soil.

Types of Graphs and Charts

Two completely different types of <u>map</u> here —
<u>topological</u> maps and <u>isoline</u> maps.

Topological Maps show how to get from Place to Place

Topological maps like this one show
<u>transport</u> connections. They're often used
to explain <u>rail</u> and <u>underground networks</u>.

It's highly unlikely you'll have to <u>draw</u> a
topological map. If you have to <u>read</u> a
topological map just remember the <u>dots</u>
are <u>places</u>. The <u>lines</u> show <u>routes</u> between
the places. If two lines cross <u>at a dot</u> then
it's a place where you can <u>switch</u> from one
route to another.

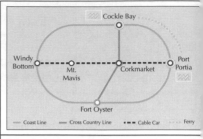
A topological map showing transport connection

Isolines link up places with Something <u>in Common</u>

<u>Isolines</u> are lines on a map <u>linking</u> up all the places where something's the <u>sam</u>·

<u>Contour lines</u> are isolines linking up places at the same <u>altitude</u>.

Isobars on a <u>synoptic chart</u> (weather map) link together all
the places where the <u>atmospheric pressure</u> is the same
(there's more about synoptic charts on page 2).

Isolines can show different things. They can be used to link up places where, s·
<u>average temperature</u>, <u>wind speed</u>, <u>rainfall</u>, or <u>pollution levels</u> are the same.

How to <u>Read</u> an Isoline Map

To read an isoline map you need to find the point you're being asked about.
Then see which isolines the point lies on or between.
You can then estimate the value for the place you're looking at.

It sounds pretty difficult but once you've seen a few examples it gets much easi·
Example:

Q: *Find the average annual rainfall*
    in a) Port Portia, and b) Mt. Mavis.

A: Find <u>Port Portia</u> on the map.
    It's not on a line so look at the numbers on the lines
    <u>either side</u>. They're 200 and 400. Port Portia's about
    halfway between, so the answer's <u>300 mm per year</u>.

    The question about Mt. Mavis is much easier.
    It's bang on the line so the answer's <u>1000 mm per year</u>.

Rainfall on Itchy Island (mm per year)
Example of an isoline ma·

How to <u>Draw</u> an Isoline

Drawing an isoline is like doing a dot-to-dot where
you join up all the dots with the <u>same numbers</u>.

  EXAMPLE:

Q: *Complete on the map the line showing an*
    average rainfall of 600 mm per year.

A: Find all the dots marked 600, and the <u>half-finished line</u> with 600 on it.
    Draw a neat <u>curvy</u> line joining up the <u>600s</u> and the two ends of the line.
    Don't <u>cross</u> any other lines or <u>go past</u> the 500s.
    The correct answer is shown as a <u>red dashed line</u> on the map.

Types of Graphs and Charts

The last kind of map you need to know about is choropleth maps.
To get the hang of them all you need to do is be able to use a key.

n Exams Choropleth Maps have <u>Hatched Lines</u> and <u>Dots</u>

nstead of using colour coding, the maps in exams usually use <u>cross-hatched</u>
ines and <u>dots</u> — because it's cheaper to print in black and white.

They're very straightforward to use, but all those lines can be <u>confusing</u>.
When they ask you to talk about all the bits of the map with a <u>certain type</u>
of hatching, look at the map carefully and put a <u>big tick</u> on each part with
that hatching, to make them all <u>stand out</u>. Look at this example, where all
the areas with over 200 people per km² have been ticked.

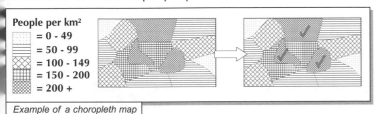

People per km²
= 0 - 49
= 50 - 99
= 100 - 149
= 150 - 200
= 200 +

Example of a choropleth map

When they ask you to <u>complete</u> part of one of the maps,
first use the <u>key</u> to work out what type of shading you need.
Use a <u>ruler</u> to draw in the lines, using the same <u>angle</u> and <u>spacing</u> as in the key.

escribing Graphs — Look for the <u>Important Bits</u>

The phrase '*Describe what is shown by the graph*' is pretty alarming.
It's a <u>nasty looking</u> question, but what they actually want you to <u>do</u> is <u>easy</u>:

The <u>four</u> things to look for:

*   Talk about bits where it's <u>going up</u>.

*   Talk about where it's <u>going down</u>.

*   If there's a <u>peak</u> (highest bit),
    write that down.

*   If there's a <u>trough</u> (lowest bit),
    write that down.

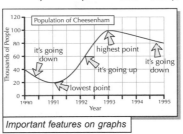

Important features on graphs

Scatter Graphs are About <u>Best Fit Lines</u> and <u>Correlation</u>

With a bit of luck, any scatter graphs will already have a best
fit line on them. If not, <u>sketch your own</u> in roughly the right
place, then write down what type of <u>correlation</u> there is:

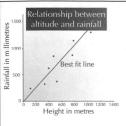

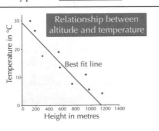

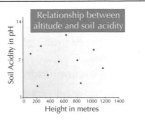

The line slopes <u>up</u> from
<u>left to right</u> — there is a
'<u>positive correlation</u>'.

The line slopes <u>down</u>
to the <u>right</u> — there's a
'<u>negative correlation</u>'.

When there's <u>no</u>
<u>correlation</u> you can't
draw a line of best fit.

The three main types of scatter graph

Revision Summary

With this section more than any other, you need to do a lot of <u>practice</u>. Obviously you have to start by learning the <u>theory</u> of how to deal with maps and graphs, but the real test is whether you can do it for real in the <u>exam</u>. The best way to see whether you can do it is to try all these questions. When you've done them once, go back and learn any bits that you found tricky. Then do it all again.

1) Complete this compass to show all four compass directions:

2) Write down the four-figure and six-figure grid references of all of the symbols marked on the map that match the key.

© Crown copyright, License no. 100034841

3) Using the above map, what is the distance, in km, from the post office to a) Manor Farm, b) Leys Barn, c) the nearest church?

4) Match each contour map with its corresponding shape.

5) a) For each point A to D marked on the map below, write down whether the area is a gentle or steep slope.

   b) Give a brief definition of a spot height and a trig point, and find an example of each on the map.

© Crown copyright, License no. 100034841

6) From the map above, draw the lake and the outline of the forest (the black line). First, copy or trace the blank grid above, then measure some of the important distances to make sure you get things in the right place.

7) What kind of features would you use to work out how a photo matches a plan of the same area?

8) Describe briefly how you would work out what part of an area had changed and why, if you had a photo and a plan of the same area with different dates.

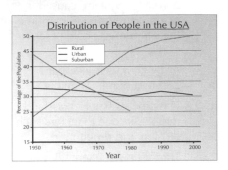

a) What type of graph is this?

b) Complete the graph to show the rural population dropped to 22.5% in 1990 and 19.8% in 2000.

c) In what year was the percentage population in urban areas at its lowest?

TIP

Go back to pages 90-91 if you're having trouble with interpreting graphs.

)

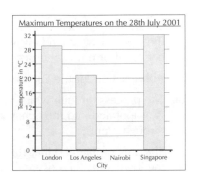

a) What was the maximum temperature in Singapore?

b) Complete the graph to show that the maximum temperature in Nairobi was 16°C.

1)

Percentage Distribution of Religions in Surinam

a) What percentage of the population of Surinam is Hindu?

b) Explain in detail how you would draw a pie chart.

2)

Pedestrian density distribution in a CBD

A
100
230 330 310
130
290
280 •325 400
300
•130   200   256   100

a) Complete the isoline for a pedestrian density of 300.

b) What is the approximate pedestrian density at point A?

EXAM TIP

There's no denying that question 14 is hard. If you're stuck, remember the 4 things which are important to mention in graph questions:

- **Talk about bits where it's <u>going up</u>.**
- **Talk about where it's <u>going down</u>.**
- **If there's a <u>peak</u> (highest bit), write that down.**
- **If there's a <u>trough</u> (lowest bit), write that down.**

3)

Life Expectancy in Southern Africa

Life expectancy in years
☐ No Data
☐ 51-55
☐ 46-50
☒ 41-45
⊞ 36-40
▨ <35

a) What sort of graph is this?

b) Describe the distribution of countries with an average life expectancy of i) less than 35, and ii) more than 51 years.

4) Describe what each of the graphs shows in questions 9 to 13.

Key Terms

abrasion	Erosion caused by rocks at the bottom of a riverbed.
acid rain	Rain that contains a high level of pollutants. It has a pH of less than 5.6.
anticyclone	A weather system of high pressure.
aquifer	A rock which can hold water that can be extracted by drilling.
arch	An archway in a cliff that has been formed by wave action.
attrition	A process in which rocks grind against each other in water to make sand.
basin	The area drained by one river and all its tributaries.
biome	A type of ecosystem which covers very large areas e.g. tropical rainforest or tundra.
biosphere	All the places on Earth which can support plant and animal life.
central business district (CBD)	The middle of a city where land prices are high. It's mostly used for offices, shops and big public buildings.
climate	A term used to describe the typical weather patterns of an area over a long period of time.
commuters	People who live in suburban or rural areas who travel daily to a CBD to get to their place of work.
corrasion	A kind of erosion where rocks get worn away by material being transported by the sea, rivers, a glacier or wind.
corrosion	A kind of erosion where chalk and limestone are dissolved in water.
counter-urbanisation	Movement of people out of urban areas and into rural areas, a trend which has increased because of an increase in commuting.
death rate	The number of deaths per 1000 people per year.
deforestation	The cutting down of large numbers of trees for wood or access.
delta	A bit of land made of sediment which sticks out into the sea at the mouth of a river, where the river splits into a number of smaller streams or rivers.
deposition	When material is dropped by a river or the sea.
depression	A weather system, caused in the UK when warm tropical maritime air from the south meets cold polar air from the north.
desert	A dry area with less than 250 mm of rain annually.
desertification	The process where grassland is turned into desert due to factors such as soil erosion and drought.
ecosystem	The system of energy flows and interactions between all the living and non-living things in one place.
erosion	Where natural forces like rivers and the weather wear land away by chemical or physical processes.
EU	Abbreviation for the European Union.
evapotranspiration	The process through which water is evaporated into the atmosphere through plants.
flood plain	The area of flat land that surrounds the lower parts of a river. It's made of sediment that has been deposited by flooding.
footloose industry	Industries which don't need to be located near to raw materials. Instead they often locate in pleasant surroundings and near to good communication links.
global warming	The theory that the average global temperature is increasing because of increased levels of carbon dioxide in the atmosphere.
greenbelt	An area of countryside around a town or city where there are building restrictions. Greenbelts are designed prevent urban sprawl.
gross national product (GNP)	The total value of all goods and services produced by one country in year, including investments from foreign income. It's often shown per person (capita) to show how the wealth is distributed.
hydrosphere	The hydrosphere is the watery part of the Earth's surface (e.g. oceans, rivers and water vapour in the atmosphere).
infant mortality rate	The number of babies that die before they are one year old per 1000 live births.
infrastructure	All of the communication structures and services in an area.
irrigation	The artificial watering of land.

Key Terms

...ching	When rainfall moves through soil washing the soluble minerals down to the lower layers.
...DC	A Less Economically Developed Country. They're also known as the 'third world' or 'developing countries'.
...ees	Raised river banks made from coarse river load material that is deposited during flooding.
...ngshore drift	The lateral movement of material along a shore in a zig-zag pattern.
...EDC	A More Economically Developed Country. Also known as 'developed countries'.
...gration	The process where people leave one place to live in another place.
...ultinational ...mpanies ...NCs)	Huge companies that have operations in more than one country. They're sometimes called transnationals (TNCs).
...ational Park	A protected area of outstanding natural beauty. National Parks are popular places for recreation and there are often conflicts over land use.
...ewly ...dustrialised ...ountries (NICS)	A group of countries which have undergone rapid industrialisation since the 1960s. NICs have a lot of foreign investment from TNCs.
...otosynthesis	The biological process through which plants make energy from sunlight and carbon dioxide.
...llution	The contamination of land, air or water with substances which harm ecosystems.
...pulation ...licies	Policies introduced by a country's government to try and control the size of the population (e.g. China's One Child Policy).
...pulation ...ramid	A bar chart used to show the age and sex composition of a population.
...ecipitation	The deposition of any form of water in the air onto the Earth's surface (e.g. rain, hail and fog).
...rimary ...dustries	Industries which collect raw materials from the earth. Examples of primary industries are mining and farming.
...ull factors	Factors which attract migrants to a place (e.g. good schools and jobs).
push factors	Disadvantages of a place which force people to migrate to other areas (e.g. crime and unemployment).
quality of life	How satisfied and happy people are.
quaternary industries	Industries that are involved in research and product development.
science park	An attractive, landscaped business park. Hi-tech, footloose industries often locate in science parks.
secondary industries	Industries where the main activity is making products from raw materials (e.g. making crisps from potatoes).
spit	A long, thin ridge of sand that extends from a beach into the sea.
squatter settlements	Illegal settlements of poorly built housing on the outskirts of an LEDC city. They are also known as shanty towns and have other names in some places (e.g. favelas in Brazil).
standard of life	The material wealth of a person or community.
stewardship	Using resources responsibly so some are left and damage caused is minimal.
sustainable development	Development which meets the needs of the present generation without compromising the ability of future generations to meet their own needs.
synoptic chart	A map which uses symbols and isobars to summarise the weather.
suburbs	Housing areas on the outskirts of a town or city.
tertiary industries	Industries which supply services to people or other firms (e.g. nursing).
tombolo	A long beach which joins an island to the mainland (e.g. Chesil Beach).
urbanisation	The increase in the percentage of a population who live in urban areas.
urban-rural fringe	The zone where the city and the countryside meet. It is a popular place for leisure activities.
water cycle	The system that links all the components of the hydrosphere together.
watershed	The boundary between two drainage basins.
weathering	The breakdown of rock by mechanical or chemical processes.

Index

Index

Index